LOOKING AT

OLD PHOTOGRAPHS

THEIR DATING AND INTERPRETATION

Robert Pols

Published by
COUNTRYSIDE BOOKS
in association with
THE FEDERATION OF FAMILY HISTORY SOCIETIES

COUNTRYSIDE BOOKS
3 Catherine Road
Newbury, Berkshire
and
THE FEDERATION OF
FAMILY HISTORY SOCIETIES
(Publications) Ltd.
2–4 Killer Street, Ramsbottom, Bury,
Lancashire BL0 9BZ

ISBN 1 85306 586 2

Produced through MRM Associates Ltd., Reading
Printed in England

CONTENTS

ACKNOWLEDGEMENT

As ever, I am grateful to my wife, Pam, who has again patiently read, questioned and commented on what I have written, and without whom etcetera...

Introduction

This book is dedicated to the proposition that the more you look, the more you see. In essence it is a casebook, offering discussion of a series of examples of old photographs. An approach to studying such photographs is considered first, but the bulk of the work is concerned with putting considerations into action by applying them to real pictures. The pictures in question are mainly studio photographs, but other kinds of picture begin to make an appearance as the years progress, just as tends to happen in any family collection. The time scale covers the Victorian and Edwardian eras and the early Georgian years, up to and including the First World War.

Faced with an old photograph, the family historian may be most anxious to sort out the who and when. Of these, the when may come first. Being reasonably sure of the date of a picture may be a help in deciding just who is depicted.

There is, however, more to be gleaned from a photograph. We may form ideas about the studio and the experience of being photographed. We may scrutinise the pose and try to interpret its subtext, whilst remaining properly wary of fancifully reading more into the image than is there.

Of course, some pictures offer more food for thought than others. Pictures from the 1890s, for instance, can be particularly uninformative. Over the years the camera moved closer to the subject when taking portraits. As it did so, potentially interesting details, such as shoes, trousers and skirts, were squeezed out of the picture. In the 1890s this closing in of the camera reached the point at which only head and shoulders were shown. Moreover, the widespread taste for the vignette, an oval of picture fading away at the edges, meant that even shoulders often disappeared from the portrait, leaving face and collar floating in whiteness. So vignettes can offer the student little evidence of clothes and none of studio to work on. For the sake of interest, both writer's and reader's, close-up vignettes are therefore deliberately avoided in the present work.

The casebook pictures are grouped according to the decades from which they are believed to originate, and an attempt is made to date each photograph. Sometimes it is not possible to be too precise, but quite often a fairly narrow span of years can be suggested — an early, middle or late point of the decade, say, or the first or second half of it. After dating, other aspects are touched on, and these vary, sometimes arbitrarily, from picture to picture. It would have been possible to discuss albumen paper, say, every time it is encountered, or to indicate the possible range of exposure times of each picture, but this would have been tedious and repetitive.

Where repetition has not been avoided, though, is in details to do with dating. This is partly because repetition increases familiarity, so that the reader, working through the book, may try anticipating what could be said, before checking it out in the text. It is partly, too, because the safest way to date photographs is to list each time every factor that can be used as dating evidence. Sometimes there are contradictory messages, with different details suggesting different dates. The more pieces of evidence one can accumulate on such occasions, the more safely and easily one can come to a conclusion about a probable date or range of dates, seeking a mean or majority conclusion. Sometimes conflicting evidence can itself prompt conclusions — that the sitter is more fashionable than the studio, perhaps, or vice versa. For these various reasons, and in the knowledge that considerations of dating are often uppermost in the family historian's mind, evidence for dating is dealt with, regardless of whether or not that kind of evidence has already been mentioned in connection with another photograph. In the same spirit, dating evidence is drawn both from the front of a picture, where it can be seen in reproduction, and from the back, where it generally can not.

An Approach to Looking

There is, of course, no one right way to go about studying a photograph. But some sense of order and method does no harm, and may help to find more of what there is in a picture. To this end, a checklist is offered. It is not suggested that there is something to be said about every picture under every heading. The list is simply a series of questions one can ask oneself when looking at a photo. Often the answer may be that the question is irrelevant. Sometimes, though, the question will prompt a profitable line of thought. The resulting checklist is not a recipe to be adhered to slavishly. It is rather a series of points to be considered as systematically or as casually as one wishes. It is put forward as an aid and not as a strait-jacket.

1. *The Type of Photograph*

What kind of picture is it? Is it a carte de visite, cabinet print, tintype, postcard, roll-film print? Is it something less common (e.g. ambrotype, daguerrotype, opal print)?

2. *The Date of the Photograph*

Does knowledge of the type of picture help with dating? Are there any clues in the type of mount and the information and design on its reverse? Can anything be learnt from the pose and composition of the picture? From the studio props, furnishings and background? From the clothes being worn?

3. *The Subject*

Can the subject or subjects be identified? Does knowledge of the probable date make one possible subject more likely than another? Can an age be suggested? If the subject is unknown, can anything be suggested about the type, class, occupation of the person? If there are two people (or more), how are they related? If the relationship is unknown, what appear to be the options?

4. *The Photographer*

What information is there about the photographer? Can a knowledge of the name and address of the practitioner confirm or refine attempts at dating the picture? Is there any sense of the photographer's status or pretensions? Is it the kind of photographer at the kind of address that you would expect a known subject to patronise? If not a professional photographer, do we know who took the picture? A friend or relative? Do we gain any sense of a relationship between photographer and subject, or any sense of the sitter's attitude to the person behind the camera?

5. *The Studio or Other Location*

What can be said about the studio? The quality of props and furnishings? The style and condition of

7

backcloth? The point where backcloth meets floor? The lighting? Does the studio seem up-to-date or old-fashioned, in view of the estimated date?

6. *The Taking of the Picture*

Was a neck support used? How stiff or relaxed is the pose? Can an estimate be made of the possible length of exposure? What sort of clothes have been worn for the sitting? Is the occasion of the photograph known (e.g. engagement, first long trousers, birthday, holiday)?

7. *The Picture as Artefact*

Is it possible to identify details of processing (e.g. albumen print, carbon print, vignetting)? What is the picture's condition? How has it deteriorated? How is it presented (e.g. frame, card mount, union case)? What is the mount or packaging made of (e.g. papier-mâché, wood, card, thermoplastic)? Is the image the way it appeared to the onlooker, as occurs when printing from negatives, or is it a reversed mirror-image, as found with daguerrotypes, tintypes and some ambrotypes? Has the image been altered, decorated or "improved" in any way?

8. *The Picture in Context*

If the photograph is in an album, does its positioning suggest anything? Can comparisons be made with other pictures of the same subject? Can family likenesses be discerned? Can comparisons be made with other pictures from the same studio?

9. *Interpretation*

What kind of impression of the sitter does the photographer intend to convey? What kind of image does the sitter appear to have of self? Does the subject appear to conform to a stereotype? Are there any suggestions of class? Social pretension? Respectability? Affluence? Where there are two or more sitters, which is the focus of attention? Where does authority lie? (Some ideas about interpretation may have been already provoked by consideration of other topics.)

10. *The Personal Angle*

If the portrait is of a relative, how does the picture speak to you? Are there any points of resemblance? What have you in common? (This is not a line of questioning that is pursued in the casebook examples which follow. Both questions and answers can only be personal. They may not take objective investigation any further, but they may hold some considerable interest for the individual.)

One final thought may be offered on the subject of studying old photographs: you never realise how useful a magnifying glass can be until you use one.

Figure 1

Everything about this carte de visite suggests the 1860s. The mount is of white card, and its corners are square-cut. Admittedly, there was some revival of squared corners in the eighties, but the considerable majority of sharp-cornered mounts belong to the earlier decade. The photographer's name appears on the reverse in a small and simple trade plate. The portrait is full-length, as was customary until the very end of the sixties, and the setting is simple, trying to look like nothing other than the studio that it is.

Though simple, the setting and pose have some dignity. The piece of furniture is substantial and ornate. Resting on it is a book - always a prop which will add a little solemnity and weight to the occasion. On this occasion the hand rests on the book instead of holding it, but the associations of literacy and taste are not diminished. The stance suggests confidence and substance. The placing of the feet seems to hint that the subject has somewhere to go. He has paused for the taking of the photo, but he is purposeful, gazing surely ahead of himself rather than at the camera.

Even the fact that the subject was shown in full-length standing pose added to the original impact, for in the tradition of portrait painting, from which photography inherited many conventions, whole-body cost more than head-and-shoulders, and therefore carried stronger suggestions of wealth and status.

The clothes belong to their time. A dark coat with pale trousers was a combination that retained its popularity until the late sixties, and the matching waistcoat did not become the norm until the mid-seventies. Rather wide coat sleeves and trouser legs also contribute to the sixties' feel. Two other details of the trousers are worth a mention. The very visible, raised seam of the trouser leg was characteristic of the decade. The turn-ups are more confusing, for they do not generally figure on fashion plates from these years. Nevertheless, in real life turn-ups were quite possible in the sixties, and may perhaps be more readily found in photographs than in fashion illustrations.

Exposures of at least a few seconds were standard at the time of this picture, and thought had to be given to keeping the subject still for long enough to avoid a blurred end-product. The furniture provides a steadying presence, but on this occasion, as on many, more help was needed, and a head-rest or posing-support was used. Its base can be seen behind the man's right foot. Photographers often used to try to conceal the evidence of head-rests, most commonly by pulling across a curtain. Instead of falling perpendicularly under its own weight, this was stretched across the picture at an angle, with the bottom

9

of the drape hiding the feet of the support. At best, such an arrangement can create a diagonal which fits in with the composition of the picture as a whole; at worst, as in *Figure 8*, it can be a painfully obvious contrivance for hiding what every Victorian viewer knew full well was there. The honesty of pictures such as this one has, perhaps, something to recommend it.

The photographer was J C Smallcombe of 33 Baker Street, Portman Square, London. A look at Michael Pritchard's *Directory of London Photographers* shows that, after first practising at 32 Edgware Road, James Charles Smallcombe could be found at the Baker Street address between about 1862 and 1869. This dating confirms conclusions already reached, but does not refine them.

The design of Smallcombe's trade plate tells us something about the professional image that he wished to project. A circle, formed of a belt, has the name running round it and a capital "S" in the centre. It is surmounted by a crown. The whole thing suggests class, echoing heraldry without being heraldic, mimicking a monogram though using only one letter, and seeming to hint at a royal association, which Smallcombe may or may not have had, but which certainly did not amount to anything so grand as a royal warrant. But the crown is, to be fair, a suggestion rather than a claim. After all, mounts frequently depicted cherubs, but no customer expected to bump into one in the studio waiting room.

Figure 2

Also from the 1860s, this carte de visite shares a number of characteristics with the previous example. The mount is square-cornered, with a small trade plate back. The pose is full length and the background is simple. Again there is a substantial piece of furniture, hinting at those virtues shared by Victorian joinery and Victorian men — dependability and solidity. On this occasion we can see an example of the popular drape, which could give some feeling of richness to an otherwise austere setting. When the curtain was not needed to conceal the base of a head-rest, it was commonly caught back, to curve gracefully out of the picture, as here. A curtain hanging loose and forming a strong vertical was less common, though not, as *Figure 3* shows, unknown.

The simple studio wall background may encourage us to think the first half of the decade more likely, as many premises moved towards the use of backcloths as the sixties drew towards their end. But though this may be a relatively early picture, there is no sign of any extra support for a subject suffering the rigours of a lengthy exposure. There is certainly shadow

around the right foot, and the floor line is curiously uneven behind the subject to his left, as if the carpet is covering something. But behind the left leg there is unshadowed and unsuspicious clarity. It really does seem to be a case of "Look, no stands". Yet the man appears remarkably comfortable. His gaze and face are serious, of course, as befits a man of

character, but they are not strained; the right hand rests lightly rather than leans on the table, the left arm hangs easily, and there is a bend in the right knee. The curtain hides nothing. All in all, it is a successful pose from an age often criticised for stiff stances and grim expressions.

Appearance and clothes reinforce our conclusions about dating. The deep cuffs and rather long trousers are consistent with the sixties. Facial hair could be worn in a variety of forms, but rarely, until the very end of the decade, as the full beard and moustache. It was common at this time for trousers to be paler than coats, and for waistcoats not to match. Here, the tiny amount of waistcoat that is visible looks as dark and unpatterned as the coat, but it is in shadow. Actual colours have, of course, been lost in the monochrome photograph, but the colour density of the clothes looks much the same all over. Nevertheless, careful inspection shows that the trousers are, in fact, a bit paler than the coat. In real life, the contrast may have been greater, since early photographic emulsions gave uncertain rendering of colours, though it was the brighter colours, more likely to be worn by women, that were most markedly misrepresented.

11

The photographer, according to the trade plate, was C T Newcombe of 135 Fenchurch Street, EC. Pritchard's *Directory of London Photographers* again proves interesting. He records Charles Thomas Newcombe at 135 Fenchurch Street from 1860 until 1873. But he lists additional premises in Regent Street between 1863 and 1867, and in Coleherne Court in 1865. It would be quite possible for Newcombe to have separately printed mounts for each studio, and some photographers did just that. Rather more seem to have listed all current studios on their mounts. This, after all, made for economies of printing and flexibility of supply. There was, in addition, a certain prestige in being able to boast of a mini-chain. The Regent Street address, at least, lasted long enough to appear on mounts. So one of the times when Newcombe ran only one studio is at least a little more likely for this carte. No mention of Newcombe before 1860 is reported by Pritchard, and a move to 129 Fenchurch Street is noted for 1874. This suggests two possible periods for 135 Fenchurch Street as sole premises: about 1860 to 1863, and about 1867 to 1873. Discussion of dating so far suggests that the earlier of these periods is more likely.

There remains one further intriguing possibility for dating. The photograph has been given a serial number, and on the back is written, in blue pencil, "8781". It would be interesting to know how long it would take a practitioner, starting in about 1860 or perhaps a little earlier, to work his way to photograph number 8781. We cannot answer with any certainty, but we can try a little estimating. Henry Peach Robinson reckoned, in the 1860s, that fifteen sitters in a morning represented a good rate of work. With good light, the afternoon could also be used, and numbers could be pushed up to twenty or twenty-five a day. Allowing, conservatively, for a five day working week, fifty working weeks a year, and four months of good afternoon light, we come up with a figure of well over 4,000 sittings a year. On the face of it, Newcombe could have reached 8781 in little over two years. In fact, many, probably most, sittings would produce more than one picture, which would reduce the period. On the other hand, Robinson was very successful, and might be in more demand than most photographers. Nevertheless, not too many years would be needed by Newcombe to reach his 8781st picture. It seems more likely that he would reach that number before 1863, than that he would not reach it before 1867, especially since the early sixties were the boom years for cartes de visite.

Figure 3

This, like the previous examples, and like most of those which follow, is a carte de visite. A paper picture was mounted on card to a finished size of about 4" by 2½", which was much the same size as a visiting card. First introduced in Paris in the first half of the 1850s, the carte de visite arrived in England in 1858, and royal interest was quickly followed by the interest of the general public. Cartes soon became very cheap, bringing portraits within the reach of a much wider section of the populace, and a craze was born. People collected cartes, exchanged cartes, added cartes of the famous to family cartes in the new albums specially designed to hold cartes. The craze was soon named cartomania, and on its back sprung up many new studios. Perhaps predictably, watchmakers, chemists, painters and printers started to offer photographic services. Less predictably, insurance men, the owner of a gasworks and proprietors of fancy goods stores tried their hand at the new profession. The high proportion of cartes de visite in this volume is a natural reflection of their importance in Victorian photography.

This example sends slightly confusing messages about its date. That it belongs to the sixties is indicated by the square cornered white mount, the simple setting and the full length shot. From clothes and appearance, though, come suggestions of both halves of the decade. Puffed upper sleeves were popular in the first half of the sixties, and the crinoline, for which the skirt seems to have been designed, lost its popularity in the second half of the period. High necklines with a small collar and brooch belonged to and spilled over from the end of the fifties. But whilst central partings were common in the first half of the sixties, the ears were generally kept covered. It was in later years that they were likely to be exposed, as here. What would seem a reasonable conclusion is that the picture dates from the second part of the decade, with a subject wearing a dress that was already somewhat unfashionable, but sporting a more up-to-the-minute hair-do. This would account for the lack of support for a skirt that was built to accommodate an ambitious but now outmoded crinoline infrastructure. (Incidentally, I feel that the skirt and the face combine to add a certain wistfulness to the picture, for both were originally intended to be more amply supported from inside.)

The move towards later sixties in dating is supported by the reverse of the mount, which represents a transitional stage in the move from the small trade plate to the overall design of the seventies. The design is still basically trade plate, identifying the photographer as Norton of 394 Kingland Road, but some additional trade information has been fitted in. Above the trade plate we

13

are told that "Copies can always be had by sending name and number", and below it we learn of "Cartes de Visite and Other portraits Copied as Miniatures or enlarged to Life Size and delicately finished in oil or Water Colour". There is a space marked "Negative No.", but this has not been filled in. A look at Pritchard's London *Directory* reinforces our attempts at dating, and pushes us to the very end of the period that is being considered, for he records Nathaniel Norton at Kingland Road only in 1869 and 1870, and practising in Goswell Road, at different numbers, before and after.

The objects on the table are interesting. One would like the equestrian statuette to be clearer, but there are no problems with the item on which the woman's hand rests. It is a union case. These hinged cases opened like a book, with two portraits inside, or with a portrait on one side and velvet padding on the other. They were made of a very early form of plastic, and, being moulded, could be covered with very elaborate and detailed designs. They were introduced in the mid-fifties, when they coincided with the rise of the ambrotype, a photograph on glass which enjoyed something of a vogue during the third quarter of the century. There is, therefore, a very good chance that the union case in this picture contains an ambrotype, though it was not unknown for the rather earlier daguerrotypes, many dating from the forties, to be rehoused in the new thermoplastic cases.

We cannot know whether the picture in the union case is simply a photographer's prop, or whether it has a personal meaning for the subject. The fact that her hand is on it creates some sense of belonging. Yet, if it were a portrait of a loved one included as a sad reminder, like the bust of the dead Albert in photographs of Queen Victoria, its talismanic significance could have been increased by having the woman look at the picture.

That this is a carte from the sixties is readily deduced from the plain back and square corners of the mount, from the full length shot, from the fashion, and from the backcloth. The full sleeves are of the time, the exposed ears suggest the middle or later sixties, but the high necklines were less favoured as 1870 approached. The most obvious fashion point, though, is the crinoline. This supported skirt is modest compared to some, and certainly a long way from the grotesque constructions which so amused *Punch* cartoonists, but it is imposing enough. The crinoline became less popular in the second half of the sixties. Backdrops showing windows looking out on country scenes tend to date from mid-sixties on. All of these details point towards the 1860s, and the mixture of late and early sixties' features would seem to invite us to settle for a point about halfway through.

Backcloths had been around since the forties, but their widespread use did not build up until later, and especially after the Paris Exhibition of 1867. Like the full-length pose, they owed much to the traditions of portrait painting, where it was customary to set the subject against a background of grandeur or classic nobility. This was designed to enhance the sense of the sitter's solvency and importance.

The woman's beads may be of some interest. They appear to be of jet. We tend now to associate jet very firmly with mourning, and certainly this association was strengthened with the intensification and codification of mourning customs which followed the death of Prince Albert. When the Prince Consort died at the end of 1861, the grief-stricken Queen Victoria plunged into deepest mourning and became (and remained) a living emblem of her own bereavement. In this as in so many other matters, royalty set the trend, and there grew up that very determined and perhaps extravagant approach to mourning that we now associate with the Victorians. The unequivocal blackness of jet made it perfect for mourning jewellery. But before taking on this identity, it had been simply a popular kind of semi-precious stone, and we should not assume, from jet ornaments alone, that a sitter has been recently bereaved. This photograph was taken after Albert's death, at a time when the public was taking up grief in a big way, but I am not at all sure that the dress looks densely dark enough to be black. Early photographic emulsions had difficulty in coping with some colours in a satisfactory way, and large expanses of black tended to come out as an unvaried, solid mass, so that sitters were advised against wearing it unless the material itself had a sheen and could catch the light. What is also certain is that red and green could come out very dark, looking quite as inky as the dress in this picture.

Thus it is quite possible that the jet in this case is simply jewellery.

The picture has been well taken. It is very likely that a head-rest is in use, and the furniture provides extra steadying, but, in spite of the several seconds' exposure, the woman has a pleasant and unpained look. The hands rest and fall, respectively, quite comfortably, and there is no evident sense of strain. The setting is good, too. The ubiquitous sixties' curtain is held back with a splendidly rich and heavy tassel, and its folds have been arranged with a care that may not be taken for granted. The furniture is solid and ornate. The painting of the backcloth has been agreeably done, with detail on the arch and in the distant trees, and with a challenge of perspective taken up in the handling of path and open window. How very perplexing, then, are the signs of carelessness. The mount has not only been very roughly cut; it has been cut to size after the pasting on of the picture. The bottom edge is unevenly trimmed. It is possible that this inexpert scissor-work has been performed at some later date. But there is no getting away from the fact that the photographer, who doesn't go in for even the simplest of trade plate self-advertisements, has been slapdash in the processing. Above the young woman's head and in the area where skirt meets table leg can be made out fingerprints from a hand contaminated by chemicals used in an earlier stage of the process.

Nevertheless, the image is well preserved. The contrast is good and there is no noticeable fading. In fact, it is often not the earliest cartes that have faded the most. In the sixties more chloride was used in the preparation of photographic paper than was sometimes the case in the eighties and nineties. The chloride attracted more substantial silver deposits during processing, and this led to greater resistance to fading. A dimly yellow picture is no guarantee of an extreme old age.

Figure 5

The trade plate on the mount of this carte names "M & Madame Szarkowska, Artistes & Photographers". Husband and wife teams were not uncommon. Nor was it uncommon for a wife to take over and run the business after her husband's death, though women operating entirely individually are less frequently encountered. There is some evidence that women's ability to put subjects at their ease was valued, and it is very likely that they found themselves behind a studio camera rather more often than they found themselves included in a firm's title. No address is given, so it is not certain that the Szarkowskas were practising in Britain, but this does seem quite possible, since their caption is in English. A fair sprinkling of foreign photographers worked in these islands, and a foreign name offered some of the romance of the exotic — a selling point not to be dismissed lightly. An idea of the perceived usefulness of foreign associations may be gained from the (generally later) practice of adopting such business names as Italian Studios, American Studios, Parisian Studios and Oriental Photo Company.

The carte bears a number of characteristics of the sixties, with a weighting of evidence towards the latter part of the decade. A full-length photo on a white card mount with squared corners and trade plate back is a familiar recipe. The skirt (full enough to have housed a now unfashionable crinoline support) and the centrally parted hair (with ears on view) combine to encourage thoughts of 1865 or later. The dress, incidentally, need not have been as dark as it seems. It may even be that the rendering of colour in early photographs has played its part in adding to the image of Victorian gloom, for reds, oranges and greens all turned out unnaturally dark on early monochrome pictures. What we may be fairly sure of, however, is that this dress was not blue, for blue took on an inappropriate pallor when photographed.

The studio also has a feel of the later sixties, with its chair for leaning on and its suggestion of outdoors viewed from within. As the sixties progressed, chairs became less often sat on, and more often objects with steadying potential and with interest in their own right. The chair here has not the heavy plushness that studio furniture was soon to acquire, though with its turning, carving, upholstering and fringing it is well on the way. It serves very well for the subject to lean on, and is probably used in conjunction with a head-rest — the pose looks relaxed enough about the arms and hands, but there seems to be a tension at neck level.

The background is something of a mixture. There is the area of neutral wall with side drape often seen in studios of the early sixties. But there is

17

also a view characteristic of later years, where parks or gardens, seen through a window or archway, combined a glimpse of rustic scene with a suggestion of classical architecture. We notice the alarming perspective of the floor depicted on the backcloth. Whilst the effect in this case is particularly disturbing, it should be noted that visual continuity between backdrop and studio floor was, for many years, not a very high priority. It appears to have been an area where the Victorians were capable of exercising a willing suspension of disbelief.

At the bottom corner of this particular backcloth, evidence of wear and tear is already becoming apparent. Signs of creasing and crumpling are not unusual. They are the result of the painted cloths being drawn into place or being wound up and down, on and off the roll. The ambitious photographer would soon build up a choice of backgrounds, rather than offer just one permanent one. Even at the early stage in backcloth history which this picture is taken to represent, there could still be a choice between backcloth up and backcloth down, and the one seen here has very clearly been moved in and out of position a good number of times already.

Figure 6

At first sight the frills and the mixture of materials and colours in this woman's dress might suggest the 1870s, when new and better dyes meant more brightly coloured clothes, and when elaboration became very much the fashion. Admittedly, the colours might not have been as contrasted in real life as they appear in sepia and white. As has been indicated, the uncertain rendering of colours in early photographs can create some misleading effects. A dress in green and blue of similar densities could, for instance, appear strikingly contrasted, with the green turning out very dark and the blue decidedly pale. A similar effect could have resulted from a combination of red and violet.

The back of the carte also gives the impression of the seventies. It is printed in gold, and the design, though basically a trade plate, has expanded to fill most of the space available, and there is a fair amount of publicity information beyond the name and address of the photographer.

Nevertheless, there are still enough symptoms of the sixties to make us pause and doubt. There are the square corners, the curtain and largely neutral

DAVID REES PHOTO.   298, CLAPHAM ROAD, S.W.

background with a hint of classical architecture, the hairstyle, the sloping shoulders and the low-set, wide sleeves. The full-length seated pose is characteristic of the decade: even towards its end, as *Figure 5* shows, chairs were coming to be used more for leaning than sitting on, and in later seated portraits the camera tends to

come in closer. But still more indicative of the sixties is the crinoline. Worn in the late fifties and through much of the sixties, it disappeared towards the end of the decade. It may well be that the style of dress is being worn at the very end of its life and that the reverse of the mount is in the vanguard of design, but we are forced to a date towards the end of the sixties, rather than one in the following years.

The chin-on-hand pose is a standard one, often used for girls and young women. Sometimes the forefinger was extended along the cheek. The suggestion was of pensiveness — a quality that was valued in a woman. Here the expression is perhaps more stern than thoughtful. As well as offering a standard and readily acceptable image of womanhood, the pose had the useful function of providing added support for the head during a long exposure. The other hand holds what seems to be a fan. This too has a double function: it is a suitably feminine, even demure, prop for a stereotype to hold, and it usefully occupies a free and potentially self-conscious appendage.

There could be additional significance in the placing of the left hand, for it enables us to see a ring on the third finger. The prominent display of a ring

19

was common in pictures taken to mark an engagement or wedding. On such occasions the couples were often, but not invariably, photographed together. This sitter may be a little matronly for a first marriage, but, in an age of early widowhood, subsequent marriages were not unusual. We can only say that the positioning of the left hand could be meaningful. A descendant might, of course, be better able to judge the degree of probability.

The picture is an albumen print, as may be seen from the typical way in which the highlights have yellowed over the years. Albumen paper was printing paper treated with a light-sensitive chemical coating of which egg-white was an important binding ingredient. For many years the vast majority of cartes de visite and cabinet prints were produced on this paper, of which the most highly valued was manufactured in huge quantities in Germany, catering for British, mainland European and American markets.

The photographer was David Rees of 298 Clapham Road and 5 Atkinson Place, both in South London. He describes himself on the mount as "Artiste Photographer" and "Miniature and Portrait Painter". Cynics may be forgiven for suspecting that artistes were thought more artistic than artists. Certainly the mention of painting is significant, for photographers were often concerned to claim that their profession was an art.

It was also helpful to be able to boast of high connections, and Rees has the royal arms depicted on his mount. He may well at some time have undertaken work for royalty, but this was not the same as holding a warrant and the right to display the arms. The list of royal warrant holders in Dimond and Taylor's *Crown and Camera* does not include his name. It seems that photographers were very fond of claiming royal patronage and the practice became so widespread over the years that eventually, in the 1880s, there was a tightening up. The firm of A and G Taylor was taken to court over their unauthorised use of royal arms and fined the token sum of one shilling. This photograph by Rees, however, belongs to a period well before the clamp down, when liberties were there for the taking.

20

Figure 7

Some of the sixties' characteristics of this carte, which are by now familiar as diagnostic of the time, might as well be disposed of first. The back is blank and the corners are squared. The setting is simple, with no backcloth, but with the use of a drape. On this occasion the drape is so firmly confined to a small corner that it adds to neither composition nor sense of richness, and achieves a convincing degree of irrelevance. Skirt, hair and ears are reminiscent of previous illustrations. The standing pose is full length, and the accompanying chair, for steadying rather than sitting purposes, may suggest the second half of the decade.

Even at the end of the sixties, supports and steadying aids remained useful, because exposure times were still likely to be of several seconds. Natural lighting through the extensive windows and, often, glass roof of a studio was still relied on, and exposures varied according to weather and time of day. At the time this picture was taken, five or six seconds of immobility might be called for on a bright morning, and perhaps twenty seconds on an overcast afternoon. There was, therefore, a need to help

L. Reali

subjects keep still, and a head rest may well have been used for this photograph. Pictures of women never have visible bases and never have drapes angled to conceal the evidence. There was no need. Women's clothes were much more useful than men's for hiding the contrivances of the photographic studio.

If extra support has been given on this occasion, a natural look has nevertheless been achieved. This derives partly from the head being turned at an angle to the body, and partly from the fact that the pose allows a comfortable slope to the shoulders. The hands each have something different to do, and the face has the desired pensive look, rather than the air of strain and apprehensiveness that was sometimes achieved. A slightly other-worldly reflectiveness is hinted at by the eyes, which do not focus on the camera, but which gaze over the photographer's left shoulder. It is perhaps fortunate that this quietly modest and thoughtful air was valued in women, since it was an air that was achievable under the conditions that prevailed. The manic gaiety expected of photographees in the twentieth century would have posed more of a problem.

Given that black would have appeared even denser, the dress is likely to be of a colour that the camera made to seem dark — red, or green, or brown, perhaps. What is evident is that the woman has taken the advice that photographers used to give, and has worn a dress of a material that has some ability to pick up and reflect the light. This may readily be seen if one looks at the right sleeve below the shoulder trim.

21

The photographer is L Reali. Though nothing is printed on the back of the carte, his or her name has been stamped from behind into the bottom border of the mount, so that it stands out in relief on the front. The name sounds foreign and the carte may not come from Britain. Whilst there were plenty of foreign photographers, or photographers with foreign names, working here, it does not seem unusual for a family album to include a carte or two from abroad. A printed back would perhaps offer a language for us to identify, but there is no such help in this case. Certainly, one would not automatically expect to recognise the nation of a picture's origin from the image itself. Study of cartes from a variety of countries only serves to confirm that there was a universality of practice in matters of costume, studio furnishings, and photographic conventions.

The focus on the face and hair is very precise. Early lenses were capable of considerable clarity, at least in those parts of the picture which mattered most. Definition might be poorer at the edges (a problem shared with some less expensive lenses today) and depth of focus could be limited, so that the background might appear slightly fuzzy.

In the earliest years of photography, practitioners tried to keep hands, the second most important features, in the same plane as the face, so crucial could a few inches be to determining whether a detail was in perfect focus or not. There may be some loss of precision in certain details of this picture, with the hem trimmings less clear than those on the shoulder, but in general one is more impressed by the quality than bothered by the minor imperfections.

Although these two cartes de visite have no known connection, they can be interestingly juxtaposed. The standing young man was photographed by Mrs E Higgins of Stamford. The sitting youth went to the London School of Photography for his portrait. The firm was, according to the reverse of the mount, based at 52 Cheapside, with six other London studios, including one in Regent Street, a fashionable location which used to be bursting with studios, and a further branch in Liverpool. It may be that some of the contrasts between the two cartes should be seen as reflecting a basic difference between the capital and the provinces.

Both pictures date from the sixties and display features characteristic of the time: white mount with square-cut corners, full-length pose, neutral background with drape. The reverse of each mount is simple, but representative of the time when the design was expanding to fill the available space. The Stamford mount has a trade plate of medium size and elaboration, with the message, "Negatives kept. Copies may always be had". The London mount offers a list of premises, nicely lettered,

and the assurance that "Duplicates can always be had". "23699" has been added in pencil. These backs, where the design begins to use up the available space whilst remaining fairly simple and sober, suggest the latter part of the sixties. This idea is reinforced by the fact that the Stamford young man is leaning rather than sitting on his chair,

and by aspects of the London studio. The full-length seated pose of the Londoner might have been on the way out in the second half of the sixties, but the painted window giving on to a rural scene was on the way in. In this case we can see only the edge of the window, with its leaded panes and with bottom half slightly open, and only a glimpse of

23

foliage to represent a verdant world beyond, but the effect is characteristic of the time. Also of the decade is the lump of classical and not very indoor plinthery serving as a hat-rest.

Both men are dressed for the sixties, with dark coat and pale trousers, and, in one case, raised side seams on the trousers. Nevertheless, the provincial subject cuts rather less of a dash. Each wears his coat, fastened by only the top button, but the resulting line is naturally emphasised by the sitting pose. The London youth's top hat, straight-sided and of medium height, adds a touch of elegance, as well as, incidentally, giving a further suggestion of the second half of the decade. The biggest contrast, however, lies in the extremities. Both heads have that rather greasy look which to us may suggest neglect, but which, in the age of macassar oil, betokened grooming. But the London hair has surrendered to control, whilst the Stamford growth hangs rather lankly on the right, and forms tufts over the ears. At the other end of the bodies, the Stamford shoes are scuffed, as can be seen on the left heel, while the London footwear has a soft and even shine.

The provincial studio, like its occupant, lacks panache. Its chair is not upholstered and has lumpy legs, whereas the capital offers a padded seat and smooth curves. The Cheapside furniture is three-dimensional and has a solid look. Mrs Higgins has a bookcase full of thoroughly two-dimensional painted books. Given the Victorian tendency to see solidity as an indication of respectability, it is easy to decide which picture sent the more impressive message.

The drapes, too, offer grounds for comparison. In each case it appears that the drape is being used, as was so often the case, to conceal the base of a head-rest. Attention is drawn to this function, in the Stamford picture, by the violent angle at which the curtain has been pulled across: the line begins near the top of the right hand edge and ends, at floor level, half way across the picture. The effect in the other picture is altogether more comfortable. To begin with, the drape is next to a window, so has a raison d'être. It performs the same concealing function, but in a much less obtrusive way: it is pulled across very casually at the bottom, without destroying the general line or losing the sense of weight of the rich material.

The feeling conveyed by sitters and studio is underlined by pose and composition. The young man in the chair has a pleasantly relaxed air, in spite of the long exposure. He sits well back on the seat, his legs are crossed, and his hand rests with fingers loosely curled under. The other young man leans with his elbow on the chair and crosses his legs, striving for ease and elegance. But crossed standing legs lack the coolness and poise of crossed sitting legs, and the result is less assured. The cane finds itself with nothing to do and simply points downwards, parallel to the right leg, whereas the left side of the body is all angles. The bent lower half of the left leg echoes the absurd line of the curtain, while the left foot turns back in at right angles to the shin, echoing the angle of the upper left arm. The effect of crowding and fuss that this creates is reinforced by the strange composition, whereby everything is crowded towards the right hand side of the picture. In the London studio, however, the visual balance is much happier: the tall curtain and window on one side of the picture are matched by the solid, heavy plinth on the other, and the subject is set between them.

All in all, when the impressions created by the various ingredients of the photographs are weighed up, it is tempting to see a contrast between provincial straining and capital self-confidence. Nevertheless, each is a striking image and has survived well. Both are albumen prints and both have become yellowish in the highlights; but both have resisted fading. The pictures are also sharp, with good depth of focus. In each case, though, there is some loss of definition at the edges of the lens, as can be seen from the London right foot, from the front of the Stamford carpet and from the top of both drapes.

There is one aspect of the London portrait which requires separate treatment, for the studio can be looked up in a directory of early photographers. Relatively few such works have been published, and not all of those are easily obtainable. Those that do exist can often help in the business of dating. Of course, many photographers worked at the same address under the same trading name for years, but many businesses appeared on the scene and stayed for only a very short time, whilst others changed hands and addresses a number of times. Thus it can happen that a particular combination of name and address, or addresses, on a photographic mount can be linked with a particular period of time.

In the case of The London School of Photography it is just two of the listed addresses that are significant, and it is Michael Pritchard's *Directory of London Photographers* that again provides the information. Though the School functioned from the late 1850s until the 1890s, premises at 23 Poultry were recorded from 1861 to 1866, and a studio at the Pantheon, Oxford Street was used from about 1865 to about 1867. Since both of these addresses appear on the back of the photograph of the seated youth, it is reasonable to conclude that the picture was taken during the overlapping period, in or very close to 1865 or 1866. Attempts at dating have already leaned towards the second half of the sixties. The directory supports this conclusion and strengthens the impression of up-to-date sitter and studio by pushing the likely time to the beginning of the half decade.

Figure 10

If *Figure 9* was a good example of the usefulness of photographers' directories, this carte shows their limitations, for the help they can give with dating relies on changes of name or address. The Stuart Brothers, whose studio at 47 Brompton Road, Knightsbridge, was the location of this picture, practised jointly at the address for nearly thirty years. A shortcut to dating is not on offer.

There are features of the carte which seem to suggest the 1860s: the corners were square, though they are now a little dog-eared; the pose is full-length; the setting is neutral background plus drape; the back of the mount is of the fairly modest trade plate type, with just a little extra information on obtaining copies. A chair being used for leaning on ties in with the second half of the sixties, though it will be noticed that this particular chair is rather plusher than previous examples, with its upholstered back and fringing pointing to a slightly later date. The card of the mount may be cream rather than white, though it is sometimes hard to decide what degree of off-whiteness should be attributed to the discoloration of age. The printing is lilac coloured, which adds to the feeling of relative modernity.

It is the costume, however, that tips the balance and demands that we nudge our thoughts towards the 1870s, the years to which the bustle especially belongs. In fact, the bustle first appeared at the end of the sixties, and its popularity waned in the latter part of the seventies, so most but not all bustles belong to the later decade. The redundant fullness of the post-crinoline skirt was caught up behind, often over padding, and allowed to fall away in sloping swathes. The resulting body shape, with its slightly tipped-forward stance, is well illustrated in this photograph, and the fact that the woman actually is leaning forward does nothing to diminish the effect. It should be added that, though this kind of sloping bustle is characteristic of the seventies, a differently shaped bustle was to enjoy a vogue in later years, and examples of this may be seen in *Figures 23* and *24*.

Also in evidence is a seventies' taste for ornamentation, with fringing at the shoulders, different material at throat and shoulders, flounces forming an overskirt and different material to trim the flounces, and some catching and incipient frilling at hem-level. Since the hair has not yet reached the elaborate and augmented excess of the high seventies, and since the epaulette effect lost favour early on in those years, it seems reasonable to place the portrait at about the turn of the decade or very soon after.

The darker tones of this albumen print have faded, but have faded evenly. The highlights are, characteristically, yellowed. The overall appearance is perfectly agreeable, but the picture, like so many, has lost much of its contrast since it was first seen. What has survived, though, is some touching in of colour. There is some pink tinting of cheeks and lips, spots of blue and orange have been added at throat and ear to indicate jewellery, and a sooty brown has been used for the hair. Colouring was quite popular. It varied from the extensive to the highly selective, as on this example. It could be done with more or less skill. Sometimes one encounters a later and ham-fisted amateur attempt to tint a picture, but professional studios commonly advertised their colouring services, and their work generally seems to have been done with some restraint and delicacy. Crude professional tinting is perhaps most likely to be seen on hand-coloured stereoscopic photos, but these are the work of production lines rather than of individual photographers with an interest in their own work.

Above the crowned, belted, monogrammed trade plate on the back of the mount is the information that the firm of Stuart Brothers was established in 1854. This was well before the boom in studios that was ushered in by cartomania and places the brothers in the second wave of professional photographers. The earliest studios were set up at the beginning of the 1840s and the daguerrotype was their stock in trade. Daguerrotypes, though, were for the fairly well-heeled, and each shot was a one-off image. It was the introduction of the wet collodion process in the early 1850s that exploited the possibilities of the glass negative and gave a significant boost to both the professional photographer and the gentleman amateur. The Stuarts were amongst those who took the opportunity that the new methods offered, and by the time of this picture (less than twenty years later) could reasonably be regarded as old hands. This photograph is numbered "67,204". The estimated average yearly turnover of 4,000 or more pictures, discussed in connection with *Figure 2*, would, if right, indicate activity stretching over about 16 years. This gives a date of 1870, which is probably not too far out.

Figure 11

Like *Figure 10*, this carte de visite hovers on the dividing line between decades. Indeed, if the woman were not present, it would look at first glance like a pretty straightforward case for assigning to the sixties. But when her clothes are looked at, and when hints from the furniture are picked out, signs of changing times must be acknowledged.

The square-cornered mount, trade plate back, full-length shot and neutral background all suggest a relatively early date. The man, too, has an air of the sixties about him, conveyed by the dark jacket with light trousers. Bold trouser stripes enjoyed some currency in those years, though they could still be worn in the seventies, as they are on the more modestly highlighted legs which feature in *Figure 13*. The top hat, with straight sides, medium height and curved sides to the brim, is post-1865, and not the first of its kind to be seen in these pages.

But the woman is dressed in the fashion of a new age and has that sloping, bustled look that appeared at the end of the sixties and was to be characteristic of a good few years of the seventies. She is, in fact, dressed very

J. BARRITT.   COLCHESTER.

much as the outdoor equivalent of the woman in *Figure 10*. Already the multiplicity of seventies' decorative effects begins to appear with the colour contrasts, fringing and banding. The age's taste for jewellery is evident in the ring, earrings, cross and chain and two kinds of necklace. Gloves are held in the right hand, and a fetching feathered hat

completes the picture. The tilting forward of hats, first seen at the end of the sixties, had two very practical advantages for the seventies. The tilt helped to accentuate the generally sloping line of the bustled look, and it provided a way of fitting both a hat and an elaborate hairstyle on to the same head. It will be seen that the hat has been tied into place by a cord or very thin ribbon that passes behind the ear and down towards the nape. Whilst the hat obscures our view of the hairstyle here, *Figure 14* may be referred to for a good idea of the way in which the seventies treated hair, like clothes, as a design challenge.

The fact that the woman's skirt, at least, is new, may be seen from the sharp horizontal creases in the panel below the gloves. Such creases, which nowadays would be anxiously ironed out, were valued as signs of a new and freshly unwrapped garment. They would drop out with wear and could not be easily replaced. While they lasted they carried something of the prestige that a designer label might today.

Having decided that the photograph shows new fashions arriving, we might also notice the studio furniture, which is starting to show signs of the padding and fringing which also characterise the seventies.

If there is by this point a strong feeling that this carte is sixties going on seventies, information about the photographer serves to confirm that view. The trade plate on the back identifies the practitioner as James Barritt of Northlight House, Colchester. A directory of North Essex studios conveniently forms a part of *The Magic Boxes* by David and John Appleby, and from this it appears that Barritt was at Northlight House, 20 Sir Isaac's Walk, Colchester, from around 1866 to about 1872. This carte would seem to date from the latter part of his time there and, once again, something in the region of 1870 is likely to be correct within a year or so.

The image has acquired a degree of mottling over the years and the limitations of the lens are shown by the fact that a little definition is lost towards the edges, with the man's foot being less sharply in focus than the faces. In general, though, the quality is pleasing, with a good range of tones, and with clear detail in both light and dark areas.

It is always interesting to consider subtextual messages about relationships in pictures of couples. The man is sitting, but sitting and standing figures can both convey a sense of dominance. Standing adds the authority of height, but those of superior rank may remain seated in the presence of their subordinates. Here, the man turns his eyes to meet the camera's scrutiny, while the woman looks straight ahead of her. The heads point in near enough the same direction, but it is the man who returns our gaze. Her hand rests on his shoulder, but in a tentative way, like one more inclined to claim sanctuary than ownership. He is master of the situation, and she is the wife whom he keeps fashionably clothed.

29

Figure 12

The neutral background of this carte might suggest the sixties, as could the drape, the full length shot and the plinth. But the mount offers evidence of new tastes. The card is cream, the corners are (just) rounded off and the design on the back, though modest, fills the whole of the available area. The wording identifies the practitioners as H and J C Burrow, Photographers, of Ferris Town, Truro, and Trelowarren Street, Camborne. By way of illustration, the initials "H & JCB" appear on a scroll. The printing, which uses seven different type-faces to convey this information, is in lilac ink. All of these features encourage thoughts of the seventies, when mount designs were becoming ornate. Counting type-faces, incidentally, can be a useful way of demonstrating to oneself that even a fairly chaste-looking design is actually showing signs of succumbing to the fashions of a new age.

One detail of the setting seems a little unusual, for pot plants tend to figure on rather later photographs and were particularly popular in the studios of the 1890s. But it might be pointed out that, in the nineties, they were used to

add a touch of the rich and exotic to the scene, and nobody would accuse the straggly growth in this picture of richness.

Men's clothes can present dating problems, for their fashions changed more slowly and less dramatically than those of women. Braid binding, for instance, caught on in the latter years of the sixties and stayed popular well into the seventies. (Much later examples are to be seen in *Figures 27* and *31*.) Broad lapels and velvet collar-facings could belong either side of 1870, and deep cuffs could suggest the sixties. Diagonally striped ties worn round stand-up collars are not unusual in portraits from around the turn of the decade. Double-breasted jackets enjoyed a degree of favour in the seventies, and the bowler hat, with its fairly high crown and parallel sides, looks as if it belongs to the same period. Later bowlers took on more of a look we would recognise as modern, whilst earlier ones had something of a sloping-sided, pudding-basin shape. Thus consideration of mount, studio and clothing gives us a selection of seventies' features balanced by a series of sixties' echoes. A date in the very early seventies would seem possible.

Before clothing is forgotten, we may pause to wonder whether there is any hint of the subject's social status. The double-breasted style came to be looked on as having a certain sporty air, but originally, as it appeared in the reefer or midshipman's jacket, it was at least partly associated with the humbler classes. The young man's trousers seem to be made of corduroy, and this particularly durable material carried resonances of work-wear. It may then be that the wearer belongs to the lowish orders.

The bent-knee, cross-legged, standing pose is reminiscent of that seen in *Figure 8*, though perhaps carried off more easily on this occasion. It aims at suggesting relaxation, like the leaning right elbow and the left hand in (or mostly in) the pocket. All the weight is put on one leg in a bid for the kind of casualness that early photographers found hard to capture. Indeed, for most subjects they would not have considered trying to catch it. It was, quite simply, not a valued quality. Such casualness in an older man would have been demeaning, and in a woman, unthinkable. But poses of this kind were not impossible for young men with pretensions to insouciance. The subtext might well be, "Look. I'm relaxed. There's nothing artificial or contrived. I have nothing to hide." But, on this occasion, what there is to hide is imperfectly hidden. Extra support was often still needed during long exposures, and it was used here. To the right of the feet is the base of a stand, and in the bend of the right knee can be seen a little of an upright that can lead to nothing other than a headrest.

Though the highlights of this albumen print have become buff, there has been no apparent fading, and the dark tones remain strong. Whilst later recipes for processing were to give more fugitive results, the printing of the sixties and seventies has often stood up well to the passage of time. This portrait, like many of its time, could easily persuade the unwary that it was newer than some pictures twenty years its junior. It is perhaps a pity, though, that the depth of tone is not all that has been preserved. Also evident, a century and a quarter later, is the photographer's fingerprint at the top right of the picture.

Figure 13

There are still echoes of the sixties about this carte de visite. The studio background is neutral, relieved only by a curtain. The corners of the mount are cut square, though by now a little blunted from handling. The back bears simply the photographer's name, presented as a signature ("Jno. Waller"), and a minimal amount of information in small print: "Photographs enlarged and finished in every style of Art". The signature, however, fills a lot of space, and though the back of the mount falls well short of all-over design, there is the feeling that we are on the way to a fuller use of space than the mere, modest trade plate of earlier years.

There is about the clothes, too, something of a feeling of transition. The tie, the cuffs and the width of lapels have much in common with those seen in *Figure 12*. The braided binding on the jacket may be hard to date, but the dark side seams of the trousers are features seen in pictures of the second half of the sixties and on into the early seventies. The fact that jacket and trousers are, as far as we can tell, of the same colour may suggest the seventies rather than the sixties, when jackets tended to be

J. WALLER, PIER PORTRAIT ROOMS, WHITBY

darker than trousers. Thus the clothes leave judgement hovering between decades. The boater does nothing to help.

Boaters first became popular in the fifties. The earliest had trailing ribbons or streamers, but when women took up this style of hat in the sixties, the men's version dropped the extra adornments.

The boater remained in favour for the rest of the century and well beyond and, unlike some kinds of headgear, achieved a kind of classlessness, being sported by wearers from all backgrounds. So boaters, unless streamered, tend to be reticent about date.

Two details push judgement into the seventies. The three-quarter length shot is an indication of passing time. Over the decades the camera gradually drew closer to the subject, and if the full-length picture is a common sign of the sixties, the exclusion from the frame of feet and, sometimes knees, tends to indicate the seventies or later.

The chair, too, is significant. It is reminiscent of the one seen in *Figure 11*, but is at perhaps a slightly more advanced stage of evolution. The seat is deeply upholstered and heavily fringed, and the flat surface at the top of the carved back is being used for its intended purpose. It has been designed as an armrest, and the chair is a studio chair. During the seventies an increasingly sophisticated array of studio furniture became available to the commercial photographer. Some items might aim to help in the business of posing the sitter; some might aim to add to the dignity and opulence of the setting; some, like the chair in this picture, may aim at a little of both. The long fringe around the seat is typical of the decade. Examples of such embellishment survived into studios of the eighties, of course, but the desire to add trimmings to furniture was a natural extension of the seventies' desire to add them to dress. In this instance, it may be that the posing chair is the latest up-to-date addition to what is still a rather modestly appointed studio.

The picture has been a little carelessly cut for mounting, as can be seen from the slightly uncertain side edges, but the image has lasted well, with good contrasts and a range of middle tones. There is a little fading towards the top, and the top right corner shows a grape-like bloom when turned to catch the light. This is caused by some of the silver content of the photographic coating making its way to the surface when gelatine, another ingredient of the emulsion, absorbs moisture.

It is worth returning for a moment to the boater. Whilst a boater says little or nothing about date or class, is does suggest something about occasion. It is summer wear, with associations of sportiveness and holiday. Whitby was, of course, a working harbour, and one to be memorably photographed in the last quarter of the century. But it was also by this time, as a look at the buildings on its north cliff will confirm, a seaside resort.

One has to guard against the fanciful when trying to interpret photographs, but it is tempting to see, in the slightly self-conscious debonair manner of the sitter, a visitor to the town who has taken himself to Mr Waller's Pier Portrait Rooms for a souvenir of the occasion. Children's holiday pictures are generally more easily identifiable, especially as the century progresses. They may have worn sailor suits, though these were not confined to coastal wear. As photographers latched on to the possibilities of the market, there was a good chance of a seaside studio providing buckets or fishing net as props for any child not already brandishing its own. But for adults at the seaside, especially in the early seventies before maritime backcloths had become the thing, there might be little more to suggest a feeling of holiday than a slightly raffish air. So, do a boater, a pale jacket, and the carefully contrived display of jewellery (at the end of the watch chain and on the right little finger) amount to a sense, albeit slightly uneasy, of panache? The reader may feel the point is being laboured; and the reader may, of course, be right.

Figure 14

There can be no mistaking the seventies' fashions worn by the two women who appear on this carte. The dresses have a mixture of colours and materials, there is a profusion of frill and ornament, and the cluttered necklines seem intent upon wrapping as many design ideas as possible around a single throat. What was fashionable in the seventies can have an alarmingly jumble-sale look to our eyes. Yet we see the costumes only in monochrome. The disturbingly assertive effect that we behold could only have been intensified by the real life range of colours. Indeed, the newer, brighter aniline dyes introduced at this time permitted an unprecedented ferocity of taste in colour.

The hairstyles add to the dramatic effect. Carefully built-up styles accorded with the tastes of the seventies and the coiffeur/coiffeuse needed some of the instincts and talents of the architect. Tresses were coiled, rolled, twisted, pinned into massy edifices, often built over pads or supplemented by false locks. There is no reason to believe that all the hair seen in the picture actually grows from the wearers' heads.

The mount is square-cornered and that, together with neutral background and drape, suggests that the sixties are not yet far behind and perhaps that the sitters are rather more fashionable than the studio. Another feature reminiscent of the sixties is the full-length shot, but thoughts about closeness of camera to subject become less relevant when two or

more people are involved. (It is good to remember, too, that many of the criteria we use for dating photographs have to do with tendencies we can observe, not rules that photographers slavishly followed.)

The photographer was Henry A Chapman of 235 High Street, Swansea, and the all-over design on the back of the mount uses a selection of type-faces to give a certain amount of trade information. Copies and enlargements are advertised, and Chapman is described as "Artist & Photographer" offering oil paintings and miniatures. (Like so many other photographers he asserts his status as an artist.) He also uses a monogram of his initials. The monogram, with its watered-down hint of pseudo-heraldry, is a common device to suggest class without having to make any specific claims. We also learn that Chapman is "Government Photographer By Appointment To The County Of Glamorgan".

The way in which he, or his assistant, has dealt with the picture is of some interest. The drape is pulled across at an angle. Photographers had learnt to do this in order to conceal the base of a head-rest. This was a useful contrivance in photographs of men, but unnecessary in the case of long-skirted women. But the notion seems to have caught on for both sexes and to have become part of the composition of many pictures. Here the curtain enters the picture at a rather arbitrary point below the top corner, slopes sharply, then disappears half-way down behind a piece of unidentified furniture. It is difficult to see its point. It might possibly be more visually satisfying on the right, echoing the head-to-knee diagonal of the seated woman.

But the women themselves seem to be dealt with quite well. Having one stand and one sit gives visual variety, whilst excessive contrast is avoided by ensuring that it is the woman who appears to be taller who has the chair. It was a common device to have the taller member of a pair sitting, so that some contrast could be achieved whilst keeping the faces relatively close together. The body of each woman is part way angled towards the other, which holds the grouping together effectively, but the heads are turned, so that the gazes converge at a point to the practitioner's left. With hands on lap, hand in pocket and hand on chair, potentially awkward appendages are occupied in a natural way.

The picture seems to me unusually free of a sense of relationship: the stander gains no authority from the extra height, and the sitter gains no rank from remaining seated. Even the hand on the chair does not seem proprietorial — merely vaguely friendly, in an absent-minded sort of way. Standing/sitting couples are often husband and wife, sometimes parent and child, and, as in *Figure 11*, a suggestion of relative status usually tends to come across clearly. Here a kind of mutual ease seems to have been conveyed.

The fuss, frills and flounces at cuff, hip, throat and hem are a firm indication of the 1870s. The rounded corners of the mounts, the simple but space-using design on the backs and the outdoor setting of the backcloth all reinforce this view. The full-length poses are a little old-fashioned, and these, together with the simplicity of the back designs, might encourage us to opt for the first half of the seventies. Thus clothes, mount, studio setting and pose all help with dating. But there is more to be said about each.

The mounts show changes of taste in more than the shape of corners. The card is cream coloured, rather than white, and the printing is in brown ink. The reverse shows, in essence, no more than a trade plate, identifying the photographer as Mayhew of 28 High Street, Inverness, but this takes up a lot of the available space. The surname is presented in script, as if a signature. The tendency for even simple designs to incorporate a variety of styles of lettering has already been encountered. The score on Mayhew's mounts is four: one style for the name, one for the street, one for the town, and one, small and at the bottom, to acknowledge the printer, Marion of Paris.

Mounts printed by firms from mainland Europe were not unusual, and examples may be seen in *Figures 18*, *19* and *21*. As mount designs grew more elaborate, mounts printed by, especially, French and German firms became more common, and printers offered a range of designs into which the individual photographer's name and address could be incorporated.

The setting is the same in each of the two pictures, except for the turning of the chair. Notice how the backcloth fades into an indistinct pallor at the centre, thus avoiding any distracting detail around the face and, in effect, framing the subject. A study of pictorial backcloths appearing in Victorian studios will show that fading, mistiness or selective impressionism were commonly used devices to prevent the setting from competing with the sitter's face.

There is a clear-cut line at the bottom of the cloth, where painted nature meets indoor floor, but such lines seem not to have worried our ancestors any more than the appearance of an unlikely chair in the middle of a woodland glade. We should see these incongruities as conventions rather than carelessness, for every age and every art has its conventions which the public is willing to go along with: Shakespeare's audience readily accepted boys portraying girls (and boys portraying girls portraying boys); cinema-goers live happily with the notion that foreigners speak to each other in accented English; and the Victorians were, for a long time at least, unbothered by improbabilities at the studio's interface of real and artificial worlds.

The studio chair was, by the seventies, more for standing by or leaning against than for sitting on. Here, turned through 180°, the chair is used to introduce a little variety into the setting. It also allows for a change of pose. The younger girl of *Figure 15* has a hat to hold. Her older sister, in *Figure 16*, is able to rest an elbow on the back of the chair in a version of the familiar pensive pose. It is, however, a slightly uncertain version, for the chair is not tall enough for her to rest her face on her hand or to lay her forefinger against her cheek. So the hand is allowed to hang, with fingers loosely curled, in the air. This may be a little uneasy, but is better by far than having the girl stoop to bring her face lower.

The girls have been referred to as sisters because the portraits come from the same source and same studio, because they may be thought to show a family likeness, and because they are dressed almost alike. It was common to dress siblings alike and children are often presented in photographs as a matched set. These two girls, approaching adulthood, have been spared the full peas-in-pod treatment. The similarities of the dresses are readily apparent, but there are differences too: a difference in colour is the most obvious, but examination of right wrists and hips will show others.

One difference, that of dress length, is significant, and might even suggest a reason for the slightly archaic full-length poses. Dress length, like hair length, was an indication of maturity. Not until adulthood did a girl wear her hair up, and not until adulthood did her hem reach the ground. Each of these girls, then, was still considered a child. But their hems are well on the way to the floor, and the longer skirt of the girl in *Figure 16* proclaims that she is the older. A close look at the two skirts will show that the lower frill of the older girl's is fully visible, whereas the younger girl's lower frill is partly overlapped by the one above it. One wonders if the dresses have been built for growth, and whether the older sister has now reached the age and height which justify hers being let down. At any rate, the full-length poses allow the senior sister's relative maturity to be asserted.

There is an interesting by-product of these poses. Look carefully at the area of shadow to the left of each girl's feet. It has a mottled look. And, anyway, should a shadow be falling just there? What we are looking at is evidence of a headrest. Posing supports were still often used in the seventies to help the sitter maintain stillness during a lengthy exposure. They are not often seen in photos of that decade, because the camera had frequently been brought closer and the feet cut out of the picture. They are not often seen in photos of women of any decade, because the floor-length skirts hid the rest's feet as well as those of the subject. But these girls are not yet quite grown-up and their skirts do not yet reach the floor. They look reasonably comfortable, and the younger one seems particularly at ease, so one's thoughts do not immediately turn to playing 'Spot the Support'. Nevertheless, a headrest has been used. The photographer has had a go at retouching the negative, not fully colouring the base out, but stippling it to break up the outline and encourage the eye to slide over the reduced and indeterminate shadow without stopping to question or interpret.

Finally, commentary on matters of detail should not make us forget the appeal of photographs as a whole. This is a rather pleasing pair of pictures.

Figure 17

It is not often that one can be precise in dating a photograph. It is even less common to be able to suggest the time of day. This example allows both dating and timing — in due course.

First, however, it is appropriate to note the kind of photograph that is being discussed. It is a tintype. A tintype was actually a picture made on a thin sheet of iron which was coated with light-sensitive chemicals and exposed (and often processed) in the camera. In the United States the tintype was generally known, more accurately, as the ferrotype, and there it enjoyed a popularity similar to that of the carte de visite in Europe. In the UK its cheapness gave it a more humble status and it seems to have been produced for the poorer class of customer or, by itinerant photographers, for the open-air, special occasion market. The picture shown here falls into the second category and is a relatively early example of that long and well-loved tradition, the beach picture.

The fact that, like most tintypes, this was cheaply and, probably, hurriedly produced is evident from the finish of the item. The corners have been cut into

rough curves and at three of them the metal has buckled. Signs of uneven chemical coating, characteristic of tintypes, are to be observed in a blistering at the edges, and a flake has broken away at the top. Also characteristic is the general darkness of the image. The highlights are grey — and mid-grey at that. Even so, this

tintype has much stronger contrasts than many. The imperfections at the corners and edges have been obscured by slipping the sheet of metal into a thin paper mount with an oval aperture. The photograph itself is pretty well carte-sized, but the paper mount makes the finished item a little larger. The back layer of the mount now bears rusts stains, reminding us that tintypes were not made of tin.

On the face of it, dating is not exactly easy. Tintypes go back as far as cartes and a shade further, the earliest dating from 1856, and they were popular, within their limits, from about 1860 until well into the 20th century. The fancy, lilac-inked design printed on the paper mount might suggest this is not from the earliest of tintype years, but that's about all. Children's clothes can be difficult to date as their fashions clung on for a long time, and favoured items such as tartan, sailor suits and straw boaters extended over many years.

Fortunately the photographer has come to the rescue and saved us from guesswork. Hand-written in pencil on the back of the mount is, "Photo by W J Frinel (or Frisel?), Cromer Beach, Augst 10th/76". The name is hard to make out. I have yet to find a photographic Frinel or Frisel in a Norfolk trade directory, but that may not be surprising. Established seaside photographers do seem to have taken themselves out and about, but many tintype photographers would have been beach and promenade operators only, and unlikely to figure in directories. There was, though, a Walter J Finch who worked in Aylsham from about 1872 to 1883, and who later practised in Harleston and Norwich. The pencilled, rust-stained name could just conceivably be his.

The picture has a pleasingly natural feel to it. Seaside photographers often set up beach backcloths in their studios, and, as time went on, offered fake rocks, bows of boats, nets, buckets and spades to create an authentic picture. But everything in this photograph is the real thing. The children are in the open, on the sand. The two younger ones look a shade worried. The boy's socks sag and the smaller girl's right stocking is wrinkled. The spades and the bucket, constructed like a small half-barrel, are for use; they are not studio props. The boat is real. The girls are dressed, as so often, alike and, boaters excepted, there are few casual concessions to the informalities of beach life, though the dreses are, for the seventies, quite simple. Their hemlines are appropriate to their junior years, and the boy's trousers are cut according to the same principle. Trousers reaching down to his shoes are a badge of manhood reserved for the future.

The sense of open-air naturalness is reinforced by the shadows. The light comes from the children's right. The older girl wears her hat horizontal rather than tilted, and the brim casts shadow on her whole face. This may suggest that the sun is quite high in the sky, albeit still a bit to one side. Perhaps an hour or two either side of noon would be a fair guess. Given that Cromer is on the north Norfolk Coast, just at a point where it is facing a little east of north, we could probably conclude that the sun is coming from the east rather than the west, and that this is a morning rather than an afternoon picture. What price about 10 or 11 o'clock?

Oh, and it was a Thursday.

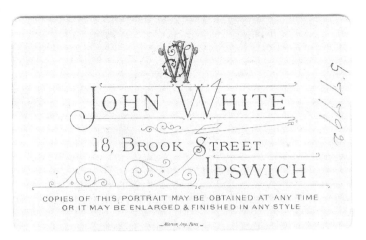

Figures 18 & 19

The backs of photographic mounts have been regularly referred to, without any being illustrated. Two carte backs, both from the Ipswich studio of John White, are now presented for consideration. On this occasion the photographs themselves are ignored. Each is of a child, and each is as datable from the mount as from the image.

Figure 18 has very much the look of a seventies' mount. Brown lettering is printed on a round-cornered, cream-coloured card. The design spreads over the space available, but is really little

more than a trade plate writ large: to the basic information of name and address are added a monogram and a reference to the possibilities of copies, enlargements and varied finishes. A monogram was, as has already been observed, a popular and relatively low-key way of adding a touch of class to the image. There is some restraint in the use of typefaces. Admittedly there are flourishes, some growing from the letters and some not, but the same lettering, in varying sizes, is used for the name and both lines of the address. The over-all effect is relatively sober. If the exuberance of clothes had reached a peak in the seventies, the exuberance of mount design had not.

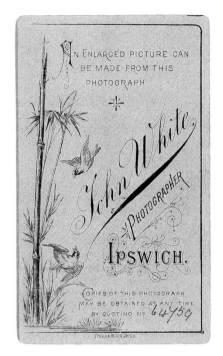

Appearances, however, can be deceptive. That this mount must date from the eighties becomes clear when the career of the photographer is traced in trade directories. John White's first discovered appearance at Brook Street is in Kelly's Ipswich Directory of 1885. Before that he had worked for a few years in partnership with Robert or

41

Alfred Cade at Westgate Street. This pairing last appeared in Kelly's Suffolk for 1883. Even allowing for the fact that directory entries were collected a long time ahead of actual publication, a John White photograph from Brook Street cannot date from earlier than the first half of the eighties. (The pencilled serial number does not help with dating, since we cannot know when the numerical series started. It may have been inherited from Walter Smith, who worked at that address from the late sixties until the early eighties.)

If White began independent practice with a slightly old-fashioned mount design, he quite soon opted for a change. 6,967 exposures later (perhaps less than two years, if there is anything to be said for the notion of a 4,000 per year average), White had a mount design with a more modern look. At first, like Mayhew of Inverness (*Figures 15 & 16*), he had used mounts printed by Marion of Paris. By the time of *Figure 19* he was being supplied by Trapp and Münch of Berlin. It has already been observed that there was nothing unusual in the use of mounts printed by overseas firms. In fact, many such mounts were not as exotic as the printer's name and address made them seem. Foreign firms could set up operations in the UK, as the occasional encounter with a mount attributed to "Marion of Paris and London" shows. Indeed, Marion & Co also operated in England as wholesale suppliers and distributors of celebrity cartes, and became the largest such dealer in the country.

White's mid-eighties mount is of grey card with rounded edges and a pictorial back that is characteristic of its time. Again we see the photographer's name, this time looking like a signature. No precise address is given, but White kept the Brook Street studio until the end of the century. We see a flurry of different styles of lettering and an assortment of flourishes, including a positive explosion of them around the town's name. But it is the pictorial element that really catches the eye.

The tradition of photography as the mirror of nature is suggested by the use of birds and a plant, though the sense of the natural is perhaps reduced by the fact that the plant is a not awfully indigenous bamboo. (Bamboo was popular though, as a wood for rustic and ornamental furniture, and, though it was in use before the eighties, it perhaps carried oriental associations that were particularly in tune with the tastes of that decade.) As for the birds, it is hard to come to any very serious conclusion. They could be intended as house sparrows, but, if so, they lack authority. The lower one seems rather contorted, but is actually reminiscent of much 19th century natural history illustration, for which the traditional source of inspiration was the museum case or drawer, and when the artist commonly worked from a dead specimen which may or may not have enjoyed the benefits of taxidermy.

Both sides, image and mount, of the same carte de visite are illustrated.

The woman's appearance suggests that this photograph dates from the 1880s. High collars with white frills became very popular, though the collar here could be a little higher for the frill to achieve the full 'pie-crust' impact. The smartness of the look was aided by the fact that the frills could often be detached for laundering. Smocked and gathered effects also came into great favour at the end of the seventies and into the eighties. The false hair of the seventies gave way in the next decade to a reappearance of the smooth head, with hair drawn into a bun at the back, as here, though the most fashion-conscious women often also wore a crimped, rather straggly fringe.

Gone, too, is the full range of decorative and colour contrasts of the seventies. This dress, rich and elaborate to our eyes, is relatively sober when compared with the excesses of previous years, though it is perhaps decorative enough to suggest the earlier part of the eighties. The contrast is gained not from juxtaposed colours and patterns, but from juxtaposed textures and responses

J. E. BLISS, PHOTO.   CAMBRIDGE.

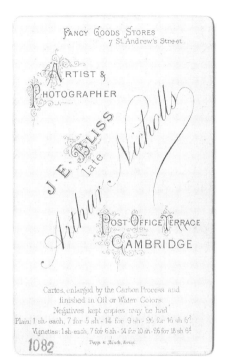

to light. This contrast of matt with glossy, of light-absorbent with light-reflecting, seems very characteristic of the eighties. Such reflective materials as satin, shiny silk, watered fabric and damasked velvet abound. These materials were not new or exclusive to the decade. In the forties and fifties the pioneer studio photographers were

encouraging women to wear satin, shot silk and heavily textured materials for their sittings, in order to avoid or relieve the density of black as it was rendered by early emulsions. Thus, materials such as these are not diagnostic of the eighties; but they are very common.

Other details, too, are broadly in keeping with the suggested dating. By

43

this time the camera was tending to move closer still to the subject. This shot, somewhere between half and two-thirds length, suggests late seventies or eighties, as does the use of the heavily padded and fringed arm-rest. The round-cornered mount, with reddish-brown printing on glossy, creamy white card, bears an all-over design which is full of trade information. It is another example of the work of Trapp and Münch, and it too would be at home a little either side of 1880.

The trade information is of some interest. The reference to finishing in oil or water colours gives an idea of the kind of services that were also offered by John White (*Figure 18*). There was some market, in those days of monochrome photography, for hand colouring. Small touches of pigment could be added to a portrait: a little red, say, on the cheeks and lips, or a touch of gold on watch-chain or brooch. *Figure 10* shows an example of a photograph which has received this kind of selective treatment. Or the whole picture might be coloured over, producing something that looked more like a miniature painting than a photograph. The prices quoted for copies seem on the high side, for many studios reduced their charges during the seventies and eighties, though a London firm which offered a dozen copies for 2/8d was unusually cheap. A shilling was, in fact, quite often the price of a single copy, but many practitioners offered rather more generous rates for six or a dozen than did J E Bliss.

This brings us to the photographer, and we find that information from trade directories leads us back to the consideration of dating. Evidence considered so far, especially that of costume, points towards the 1880s, and perhaps to the first half. Reference to the author's own directory of Cambridgeshire photographers makes the earliest part of the possible date range seem the most likely.

John Bliss succeeded Arthur Nicholls at Post Office Terrace towards the end of the seventies, first appearing in Spalding's Cambridge Directory for 1878. By 1881 he was advertising the two premises, but Kelly's Cambridge for 1883 records him only at St Andrew's Street. Exactly how far either side of 1881 he held the two addresses is not known, but already there is enough to show that this carte must date from the very late seventies or very early eighties.

The mount's reference to Nicholls, in a print larger than that used for Bliss' own name, suggests that Bliss was still leaning significantly on the reputation and goodwill of his predecessor's business. It may be that Nicholls' name was worth making something of. Nicholls himself had been one of a number of similarly named photographers in the town. At least three other holders of the name provided him with competition during his career, and one of them, William Nicholls, had been one of the county's earliest photographers and its first identified licensee for the daguerrotype process. Arthur, it seems, had been keen to disassociate himself from other Nichollses and, during the sixties, advertised himself as having "no connection with any other house". So Arthur Nicholls may have passed on a jealously guarded reputation to John Bliss. But Bliss would surely only trade so heavily on the other man's name, writ larger than his own, while himself becoming established. After a little while one would expect the former proprietor's name to be at least reduced to second billing. Thus the picture seems likely to belong to the very early stages of Bliss' career. The serial number would seem to add weight to this conclusion, for it might take only months to clock up a thousand exposures. The numbering system could, though, date from the acquisition of a stamp, rather than from the first-ever sitting. All in all, if we settle for 1880, we seem unlikely to be more than a year or so out.

A final few words might be said about the image itself. The pose is comfortable: the woman leans easily, her attention directed away to the photographer's left, with a slight smile on her face. Her expression gives an indication of how exposure times had changed. While still much longer than the fractions of a second that today's subjects are used to, exposures were, by the eighties, short enough for a reasonably relaxed expression to be held. Sitters refrained from broad smiles, not because the technology was not up to it, but because calmness and dignity were still the qualities that were valued. Looking mildly agreeable and at ease might be acceptable, but levity was another matter.

Lenses had improved, too, and depth of focus created few problems. Here, the precise rendering of the hair is matched by the well-captured texture of the upholstery material, which is nearer to the camera than is the woman's head. In earlier years, photographers had striven to keep as much of the subject as possible in one plane, in order to keep everything in focus. But there could still be some loss of definition at the edges of the lens, as can be seen by looking closely at the fringing.

Figure 22

This is an example of a cabinet print, a format first produced in the mid-1860s in an attempt to corner a share of the photographic market at a time when the carte de visite was showing signs of falling away from its enormous and unsustainable peak. The attempt was successful, though the carte continued to flourish for many years and it was not until the 1890s that production of cabinet prints exceeded that of cartes de visite. The format is recognised by its size: the print measures about 4″ by 5½″, and the addition of a mount brings the finished size up to about 4½″ by 6½″.

Trends in photography were, from its earliest days, on an international scale. The English use of French and German mounts has already been seen. German photographic paper was in common use throughout Europe and in the United States. Both the daguerrotype and the carte de visite were French in origin, but neither stopped in France. As a result, the fashions we see in studio furnishing, poses, formats and mounts tend to hold good, regardless of a photograph's country of origin. Many British family albums contain pictures from abroad, especially of relations who have emigrated or who have pursued a career in Europe, New World or Empire, and often it is only details printed on the mount that reveal this fact. There can be some differences of clothing or hairstyle, but even the people themselves often look remarkably similar to their relations who stayed at home.

This cabinet print comes from a French album and is the work of Monsieur Nys of 20 Rue de l'Hospice, Roubaix, but it can, to a great extent, be discussed in the same way as any home-grown example. The cream mount with rounded corners and brown printing, the back-filling design, incor-

P. NYS   ROUBAIX

porating trade plate and trade information, and the matched dressing of siblings are all familiar. So, too, is the relating of skirt length to age, with a distinctly short skirt for the youngest girl on the left and one that approaches but does not reach full length for the older girl on the right.

Fashion details belonging to the eighties are well in evidence. Bodices are buttoned to the throat, there is a degree of post-seventies severity of style, and the decorative emphasis is on the upper half of the body. The decade's taste for tailoring is apparent in the two-piece or trompe l'oeuil dresses and in the use of pleating. Pleated skirts were especially popular in the earlier years of the eighties, to which this picture probably belongs.

Some aspects of the picture are worth comment. The fact that it is a full-length shot is of no particular dating significance, for conventions regarding closeness of camera to subject tend to be less applicable to both children and groups. But the handling of the group is of interest. The arrangement of children close together round the table, with heights ascending and descending, and with each body overlapping or over-lapped by another, gives a firm feeling of unity. Within that, however, there is a strong sense that we are looking at two pairs. The two older girls have their own thoughts, and their eyes are directed away to their left. They are next to each other and the hands of one rest on the chair of the other. The two younger children are close together and both look steadily at the camera. Even the facial resemblances seem strongest within pairs.

Visible hands are well occupied with chair and books, and the books are deployed, one held open, one with finger kept in the place, as if they are for use rather than for sitter management. There is some good, solid furniture with fringing, carved detail and rich, heavy tablecloth all adding to the sense of prosperity and class. A backcloth de-picting an interior scene could belong to any decade from the sixties on, but the quality of this one is far from routine. The architectural detail adds to the general air of distinction, there is a well-managed sense of depth, and the perspective is good. The lighting from the window on our left is in accord with the real studio lighting, as we can see from the shadows on the tall girl's face and the seated girl's skirt. It is as if they are lit by another window, out of our view, but in the same wall as the one we can see. One way and another, it's a classy picture. A modern eye may regret the visible line on the right, where backcloth meets floor, but this, as remarked elsewhere, was a studio convention that our ancestors seem to have taken in their stride.

The reverse of the mount boasts of "Photographie instantanée" and "Photographie inaltérable au charbon", and claims "On opère par tous les temps". By the eighties exposures were short enough to at least seem instantaneous, and electricity had started to make it possible for photographers to keep working regardless of gloomy weather, (though some practitioners were slow to introduce electric light to their studios, judging it too harsh). As for the carbon printing process, that had been available since the 1860s, though albumen printing paper retained its dominance for many years. It is generally alleged that carbon prints can be identified by a slight relief effect when the print is held at an angle. I have to confess to frequent difficulty with seeing this. More easily observed are the rich sooty browns, the lack of yellowing in the highlights and the good tonal gradation, such as can be seen here in the range of tones of the backdrop and the dress of the girl on our right. Carbon prints could also, incidentally, be produced in red, blue, green and black, but a fuliginous brown seems to have been particularly favoured.

47

Figure 23

This woman, leaning forward with forefinger extended along the side if the chin, is arranged in a stock pose. The suggestions of proper womanly stillness and pensiveness have been encountered before, and we recognise that we are looking at a stereotype.

The cabinet print on which she appears is French, and from the same album as *Figure 22*. But, though the printed language of the mount is French, in other respects the photograph speaks in a sort of visual Esperanto and we can discuss it without difficulty.

The mount is of white card with purple printing. The all-over design of the back, whilst simpler and less cluttered than many, displays variously ornate styles of lettering and finds room to proclaim the competitive successes of the practitioner, Gustave of Le Mans. It lists and depicts the gold and silver medals of the Grand Diplome d'Honneur won by him in Paris and St Dizier in 1860, London in 1872 and Le Mans in 1880. Such reference to competitions, exhibitions and awards became common practice amongst studio photographers. Success was good for the image. The natural tendency to boast of it often serves, as on this occasion, to remind us that photography had an international dimension. Here we have a French photographer gaining recognition in London. Examples of British photographers making their mark abroad are not hard to find. In the mid-eighties, for instance, the mounts of Alexander Henderson of London illustrated medals won in Paris and the United States alongside the medal of the Royal Cornwall Polytechnic Society. Gustave's reference to his Le Mans award does, of course, conveniently provide an earliest possible date for the photograph.

The picture is vignetted, fading away to white at the edges. This might perhaps encourage our dating thoughts towards

the nineties, when vignettes were enormously popular. But nineties' taste was especially for the head-and-shoulders vignette, which this is not, and the technique was not, in fact, exclusive to the decade. Henry Peach Robinson was producing and advertising vignettes in the late fifties. As we move through the eighties, the beginnings of a fashion-snowball can be seen. In the nineties this became something of an avalanche, and the vignette became so depressingly common that it is true to say that the vast majority of vignettes have to date from that decade. But they were possible before, and that this one is earlier is hinted at by the two-thirds-length shot, and proved by the fashion details.

The figure-fitting bodice buttoned to the throat, with standing collar and pie-crust frill (and, incidentally, matching cuffs), is very 1880s. The hair is centrally parted and pulled back, but either side of the parting it falls forward in the tousled fringe that was popular in those years. But the key feature is the bustle, which is not the sloping construction of the seventies, but a new, higher version, jutting out from the small of the back before falling away sharply. The bustle enjoyed two incarnations: first, in the late sixties and first half of the seventies, as a sloping sweep of swathed and padded material, and secondly, during the first half of the eighties, as the shelf-like protrusion seen in this portrait. It is this detail of clothing that enables us to place this picture in the early or middle part of the decade.

The high bustle, of course, gave a very distinctive shape to the figure. In this particular case, though, we find on closer examination that the characteristic line has been exaggerated by a little retouching. The curiously stippled effect of the background behind the small of the back and just above the bustle suggests that the negative has been 'improved'. A crescent-shaped slice of the back, which appeared white on the negative, has been dotted in darkly, in order that it should appear pale, like the background, on the eventual positive print. As a result, the subject has been slimmed down and the fashionable shape accentuated. The stippling technique used for retouching was not so very different from the technique of pointillism, which was first exhibited at much the same time as this photograph was taken, also in France, in Georges Seurat's 1884 painting, 'La Baignade'. (This is, of course, just an agreeable coincidence, laboriously pointed out, and not a discovery about the historical interdependence of painting and photography.)

This carte de visite has a black, round-edged mount with gold lettering. The printing of the photographer's name and address, J B Duffie of 1 New Brown Street, Manchester, is slightly impressed, and the edge of the mount is bevelled and finished in gold. The back is entirely plain. Dark coloured card, gold printing and impressed lettering all tend to be signs of the century's last decade, though all began to be seen during the eighties.

That this is a fairly early example of such a mount is indicated by the woman's appearance. The jacket is tailored, and the collar is high and fastened to the throat, with the resulting faintly military (or, perhaps, riding to the hounds) look which commonly signifies the eighties. She wears a high bustle of the reincarnated, sticking-out kind. Her crimped and tousled fringe, so curly that it rises off the forehead rather than falling on it, belongs to the same period. Fringes became popular in the 1870s, in imitation of Princess Alexandra, Princess of Wales. By the eighties women were looking on the fringe as a feature to do something resourcefully

decorative with. In the nineties fringes were rare.

Thus evidence of fashion shows this picture to date from the 1880s. Since the second-generation bustle lost favour in the second half of the decade, the photo is likely to be not much later than 1885. The nature of the photographic mount, however, suggests that the picture is not

much earlier. Mid-decade is probably about right.

It will be noticed that the fashion in skirts produced changes in other items of clothing. This woman's jacket has been cut to accommodate her bustle. Bustle technology had moved on since the horse-hair (or even old newspaper) paddings of the seventies. Supports of the eighties were often proclaimed 'scientific'. A wire mesh contraption, marketed as the 'Health Bustle', was advertised as being less heating for the spine. The 'Langtry' adjustable bustle folded up when sat on and sprung back into shape when the wearer stood up.

Victorian studio photographers are often criticised for producing routine and uninspired work. It is possible, though, that "routine and uninspired" may sometimes be another way of saying "workmanlike and competent". It may be appropriate to consider what, in this unremarkable portrait, the photographer has actually achieved. The woman, dressed in her Sunday best, nevertheless looks reasonably at ease. Shorter exposure times by the mid-eighties made being photographed a more comfortable business. The camera is far enough back to make something of an impressive skirt, though it is arguable that the slightly pouchy bottom fold at the front could have been excluded from the frame. The hands are naturally occupied: one lightly clasps the other, and both rest, rather than lean, on the back of the chair. The incidental outcome of this is that a pair of new, heavily ribbed, supple (and probably not cheap) leather gloves are displayed. The body and head are at an angle to the camera. Thus a front view of what may be a rather full face and the profile of what may be quite a heavy nose are both avoided. It seems likely that the best angle has been selected.

The setting, too, serves its purpose. The heavy, turned, upright chair has thick, brocaded padding and tassels you could hang a swing from. Its solidity and richness are just the qualities that society valued and that the photographer aims to project. Two more hefty pieces of furniture appear on the painted backcloth, though only one is seen in any detail. Again, the aim is to give the impression of a substantial and solvent world in which the client is at home. The

sitter is dressed for an occasion and the studio provides her with a suitably dignified and weighty setting.

When we review the result as a whole, it has to be admitted that there's nothing special or clever about the result. It is, perhaps, routine. But it's perfectly all right. Originality is not what was required. The photographer has done what he has set out to do and has produced a successful studio portrait.

Figure 25

This cabinet print is mounted on white card, with gold imprinted lettering on the front and green ink used for the all-over design on the reverse. Both front and back show a coat of arms over the motto "Let Glasgow Flourish". Claims of photographers to royal patronage, artistic stature or competitive success have already been mentioned. Another fairly common way of projecting a prestigious image was to promote, as here, a sort of civic status, using badge, arms or picture of a local landmark.

Whilst women's costume often gives an immediate idea of decade, or even half decade, men's clothes can be particularly difficult to date. To say that they were less fashion-conscious might be to partly miss the point. Perhaps we should think of steadiness, reliability, and a distrust of the ephemeral as virtues making up the fashion-statement they wished their appearance to present. Certainly, though, aspects of men's clothes persisted for years. As a result, it is often helpful to form a preliminary idea about date from other details, and then to check that the clothing is not inconsistent with the conclusions reached.

The mount proves helpful in moving towards a date. The gold and green printing and the back's pictorial design belong to the eighties or nineties. The back shows the coat of arms again, displays the photographers' name once on a scroll and once, with a flourish, above the studio address. It includes room for a serial number, and informs us that "Copies can always be had". But most striking is the picture of a young woman, swathed in flowing robe, apparently floating in the air, wearing a cap (the cap of Liberty?), with a star shining above her head. Her left hand bears aloft a laurel wreath, while her right carries an artist's palette, brushes and rest. If there can be such a thing

Hampton   195½ ARGYLE ST
GLASGOW.

as a visual mixed metaphor, it is she. The mount must belong to the eighties or later. Two details, however, must be accounted for. The full length pose is reminiscent of the sixties - but how else can the carefully shined shoes be featured? Also apparently sixties-like are the mount's square-cut corners. But there was, in the eighties, something of a revival of squared corners. Many mounts were still rounded off, but squared ones did make a limited and temporary comeback. Thus, though at first sight an apparent problem, it is the corners, together perhaps with the fact that the mount is of white rather than coloured card, that lead us to assign the picture to the eighties rather than the nineties.

When the clothes are considered, they fit in well enough with the dating that seems likely. Matching waistcoats became the norm in the late seventies. The relatively straight, narrow cut to the clothes seems appropriate to the eighties. (From the end of the decade and into the nineties suits often looked baggier.) The tie with large and rather loose knot, the prominent near-to-centre parting, the turned down collar and the waistcoat with lapels are all consistent with, but by no means exclusive to, the eighties.

It happens that Glasgow, where the photograph was taken, is one of those areas for which information about early studios exists. Michael Hallett's *Victorian and Edwardian Professional Photographers in Glasgow* shows that the Hampton Brothers were recorded in, and only in, 1883 at three different Glasgow addresses, including 195½ Argyle Street. From 1873 to 1882 Alfred Howell was practising at that address, whilst the Smith Brothers occupied the studio in 1884 and 1885. The gap between collecting information and actual publication of trade directories means that dates derived from them have to be treated as approximate, so 1882-1884 seems a reasonable date range for this cabinet print.

This photograph, like *Figure 23*, presents us with a stereotype. The stern and purposeful stance, the clenched right fist, and the firm jaw, accentuated by a slight tilt of the head, all speak of manliness. The slight upward cast of the eyes suggests that manliness is tempered by thoughtfulness, perhaps even idealism or spirituality. The watch-chain and the shiny shoes suggest the sort of solid respectability which the studio furniture would also like to convey. Unfortunately the chair and occasional table rather hem the subject in, and the drape, though rich and heavy, obscures most of the table and helps to create a sense of clutter. The backcloth, with its second curtain and its painted foliage, does nothing to relieve the effect.

The white mark curving down the picture, from left eye to barley-twist chair-leg, is a scar caused by the page of the album opposite to the one in which this picture is normally housed. Over the years the edge of an oval pre-cut aperture has pressed against the photograph, giving rise to a very evident abrasion. Album scarring is not especially uncommon and is sometimes the explanation of marks on now loose pictures that have strayed from their original housing.

Figure 26

The black mount of this carte de visite is printed in gold and, like *Figures 19 & 21,* is another example of the work of Trapp and Münch. The reverse bears the photographer's name and address, promises that copies may be had by quoting the serial number, and includes, as well as decorative scroll-work and bordering, two pictorial elements: the royal arms and a set of Masonic symbols.

The coat of arms is large and central, and features a slightly irritated unicorn and a rather mumpish lion. To be justifiably able to claim royal patronage was, of course, good business. To appear to claim royal patronage or to claim it unjustly also seemed a good idea to many. Whatever work Frederick Cole may or may not have done for the royal family, he does not seem to have been entitled to use their arms for, like David Rees (*Figure 6*) he is missing from Dimond and Taylor's list of warrant holders.

The use of Masonic symbols, dividers and square encompassing the sun, may have been more legitimate, and Cole presumably saw it as a useful way of soliciting the interest of fellow members, but it still seems a little

F. COLE PHOTO.   378 EUSTON ROAD N.W.

surprising to find such open use of these images for what amounts to advertising purposes. Perhaps, though, a lack of reticence that would be frowned upon today was more acceptable then. One very popular and widely purchased carte showed the Prince of Wales in his regalia, it was not unusual for men to be photographed in the trappings of

membership or office, and Cole was not the only photographer who made free with the symbols of the fraternity in his publicity.

A scrap of tissue paper adheres along the top edge of the back of the mount. This is all that remains of a flyleaf, designed to fold over and cover the photograph itself and sometimes used to protect the image. Hardly robust by nature, the flyleaf often suffered when the carte or cabinet print was inserted or withdrawn from an album aperture. Some flyleaves survive, often hidden in albums, and waiting to tear when somebody attempts to extract the picture. A thin strip of tissue or a thin strip of glue is more often all that remains by way of evidence.

A dark mount with gold lettering is often a sign of the 1890s, but earlier examples are encountered, and it is the clothes of the women that assure us that this carte belongs to the 80s. The tailor-made suit was a significant new fashion phenomenon of the age. Many had the markedly military look that double-breasted jackets, high collars, braid and frogging helped to create. Hats piled up on top (like walnut whips, or socially climbing cabbages?) can be found in fashion plates of the mid- and later eighties, as can sleeves which are slightly short of full-length. Each woman, as befits the fashion-conscious, wears a fringe, one straggling somewhat, the other tightly curly. The younger woman's jacket seems to be cut to accommodate a not quite visible bustle, which encourages us to look no later than the middle of the decade. Above-the-wrist gloves, worn by one and held by the other, and an umbrella are accessories to complete the picture.

Pritchard's *Directory* informs us that Frederick Cole's studio at 378 Euston Road, his fourth studio, was active during the period 1883 to 1908. This supports our inclination not to place the picture too early in the eighties. The fashions, on balance, prompt us to opt for the middle of the decade, whilst the mount nudges us towards its later years. There is one detail, though, that encourages thoughts of Cole's earliest years at the Euston Road address, and that is the use of the royal arms. The private prosecution brought against A & G Taylor for unwarranted use of royal arms took place in 1884, and whilst it produced only a token punishment, it seems to have succeeded in discouraging the taking of liberties. If Cole was using unauthorised arms after 1884, he was being bolder than most of his colleagues.

What, finally, is to be made of the image itself? The closeness, the touching and the relative ages suggest mother and daughter, and the hand-holding and arm round shoulder are warmer and more informal than is usual. The daughter, if that is what she is, seems protective. Could they be in mourning? The clothes are dark, and may or may not be black. They are wearing light veils, discernible from what at first look like faint scars at nostril level. The mother's face, in particular, is solemn, though solemnity was still the norm. There is a rather dull, coarser-textured panel down the side of the daughter's skirt, which looks like mourning crêpe. I find myself coming back to the body language. Often daughters, even grown-up ones, show by their body language a subordinate relationship to their parents. Here it is the younger woman who dominates. But she seems to do so solicitously rather than authoritatively. Readers are invited to come to their own conclusions.

Figure 27

It is tempting to pretend to cleverness in dating this carte de visite. One could argue that the cream mount, printed in a colour somewhere between aubergine and brown, and embellished with varied and fancy lettering and pictures of a bamboo plant and flying swallows, must belong to the last 20% of the century. One could point out that, despite the difficulties of dating men's clothing and the fact that braided lapels and cuffs can be found in photographs throughout the period under discussion, high shirt collars were very much a feature of the nineties. One could observe that vignettes, of which this is an example, are highly characteristic of the same decade.

But why not be honest and admit to a gift of information gratefully received? The photographer, J S Tulley of 24 to 30 Division Street, Sheffield, was in the habit of having a date printed on the top right-hand corner of the back of his mounts. This example bears the date "1890". Would that more photographers had followed this practice. But then, it hardly seems fair to blame Victorian photographers for failing to provide a date, when our own ancestors, and

TULLEY & C°   SHEFFIELD

possibly even we, have often failed in just the same way.

It is, of course, reasonable to conclude that the picture dates from 1890 or very soon after. The use of such mounts at any more than slightly later date would, after all, be counter-productive, suggesting a using up of old stock and the failure of business to be as brisk as

expected. We may infer, therefore, that J S Tulley's studio was flourishing. The premises were, the address suggests, quite extensive, and turnover was high enough to warrant frequent new mount printings. Tulley was also concerned about keeping up-to-date in other ways. A carte from the same album, dated 1882, has a simpler design but the same address. What it lacks, and what Tulley had acquired eight years later, is National Telephone Number 219.

A vignette is an oval or occasionally circular image fading to whiteness at the corners and edges of the print. The technique was used at least as early as the 1850s, but it came to dominate studio portraiture in the nineties. The earliest examples involved blackening a piece of glass over a candle frame, so that it would exclude light, and placing this over an exposed plate, which was then exposed a second time. This gave a negative with overexposed outer edges, which appeared white on the subsequent positive print. A later and typical process used a glass slide with an opaque centre. This could be slipped into the camera for the second exposure, and it cut out the extra trip to the darkroom.

Vignette portraits are usually of head and shoulders only, but, since these show us little of costume and nothing of background, examples involving longer shots have been chosen for this casebook. Tulley produced standard vignettes, as a traditional close-up picture on another 1890 mount in the same album shows. Here, however, he has drawn the camera further back, and it is the fading away of the man's legs and the seat of his chair that shows vignetting has taken place.

Enough of the chair is visible to indicate that it is elaborately upholstered, with a gloriously useless froth of macramé hanging from the arms. It is a typical piece of studio furniture, though of a kind more often seen in pictures of the seventies and eighties. This may not simply mean that furnishing fashions changed. It may, at least in part, be because the furniture on which nineties' subjects sat was frequently excluded from the picture.

The man himself cuts a comfortably authoritative figure. He is at ease, with hands relaxed and legs crossed. His lips are very slightly parted, as if he is about to speak. The pose is effective and the portrait is an example of a decent, unexciting, routine, professional job. Nothing wrong with that.

Or nothing much. A book is used, as so often, to add a touch of scholarly dignity. I can't make out the title with any certainty, but think it may be *The Tablet*. A forefinger retains the place, as if to suggest the serious-minded sitter has obligingly paused for a portrait before resuming his earnest studies. But the finger in the place need fool nobody. Unless the title has been printed low down and (if I am right about *The Tablet*) the wrong way up on the <u>back</u> cover, the book, that he has supposedly just broken off from reading, was being read upside-down.

Figure 28

This vignetted cabinet print has a black mount imprinted and edged in gold. This is characteristic of the strong taste in the 1890s for dark coloured card with pale lettering. Gold, or perhaps white, was constantly set against a background of, especially, dark green, maroon and black. Though nineties' backs were often highly decorative and fancifully pictorial, examples of undecorated backs are not uncommon amongst these dark mounts. In this case, the reverse is plain black. Thus the combination of mount and vignette format point firmly to the picture's decade.

The studio setting also indicates the later years of the century. The backdrop is very indistinct and largely lost to the vignetting. This is rather a pity, as it looks elaborate, with a romantic mixture of foliage and architecture and, perhaps, the sort of outdoor artificiality that was common in the 1890s. Plinths and balustrades had enjoyed some favour as early as the sixties, but such early examples generally have a bland, new and rather cardboard look. Studios of later years saw a revival of such garden structures, but in the more weathered and rustic form that is seen here. The highly textured look of the mock-stone is typical of the eighties and nineties. Plinths like this one, with the lion's head motif, were popular. They could be provided in sections that could be assembled and reassembled so that changes could be rung and height altered. A carte of a standing man, from the same studio and period, shows this very plinth turned through 90° and with an extra block added between body and base, in order to make it high enough for an adult to lean against. A different, slightly oriental backcloth was used on that occasion.

The lad has a very self-assured air. As far as he is concerned, there is nothing modern or disconcerting about photography. He has grown up in the age of shorter exposures. His cool gaze suggests ease, as do the feet, which can be safely crossed without any fear that a slight wobble will lead to a blurred result. Leaning on the plinth, in the 1890s, could be done for casual effect rather than for support. He feels grown up, and the possession of a watch chain (and, presumably, a watch) marks his progress towards manhood. He has some way to go yet, though, as the length of his trousers indicates. His collar might better be described as Harrovian than Eton, since it is worn outside his jacket. Less modest versions of the Harrovian collar may be seen in *Figure 36*.

The photographer, Jasper J Wright of King's Lynn, practised at 125 London Road from the late eighties until the time of the Great War. He succeeded Robert Wright, who had moved into the premises in the early seventies and had, for the first few years, combined his photographic studio with a china and glass warehouse. It was common for early photographers, perhaps tentative about putting all their eggs into the one new art, to keep two businesses going. By Jasper's time, however, the London Road enterprise concentrated on photography and was the centre of a thriving mini-empire, with branches, at various times, around west and central Norfolk and in Cambridgeshire and Lincolnshire. He seems, though, to have routinely used the one address on mounts from his Lynn studio, so there are no details of the current state of his chain to help with the dating of his pictures.

At the beginning of the decade Wright was charging upwards of 8/- a dozen for cabinet prints such as this. In an 1895 advertisement he offered himself as a specialist in children's portraits, which could be taken for no extra charge. Earlier studios often charged more to photograph children, because they found it hard to keep still for the required time and the chance of a spoilt plate was so much greater. Some asked extra to photograph the under-eights; others penalised only the under-fives. Prices could be as much as double. Other practitioners made a virtue of their willingness to accept children at standard rates. The occasional wasted plate could be set against the possibility of continuing custom from the family. Nevertheless, by 1895 the problems of infant photography must have been well past their peak, and I can't think that Wright was being unusually generous.

An enthusiastic musician as well as a photographer, Wright appears holding a string bass on an 1894 photo of King's Lynn's first Town Band. His favourite slogan, which was used in a number of his advertisements over the years, remains good advice to all photographers and family historians: "Preserve the Shadow ere the Substance Fade."

Figure 29

The mount of this cabinet print is readily ascribable to the eighties or nineties. The cream card is printed in gold on the front, and in brown on the back. To name, address and trade information, all presented in a welter of typefaces, are added a central line drawing of assorted flowers (of which thistles are the most easily recognisable) and geometrical patterns in three corners. The fourth corner boasts of a prize medal won at the Photographic Exhibition of Great Britain in 1878, and of the only gold medal presented at the International Photographic Exhibition of 1880. The mount was printed by Alex Lindner of Berlin. The photograph was taken by Augustus W Wilson & Co., of 13F Dalston Lane and 77 De Beauvoir Road, Kingsland, London.

The gold medal reference gives an earliest possible date of 1880. A look at Pritchard's *Directory* pushes us, if confusingly, towards a rather later date than that. He records the De Beauvoir Road studio no later than 1894 and the Dalston Road address no earlier than 1899. He also notes a studio at Liverpool Street between the two, in 1896. If we regard the Liverpool Street information as neither here nor there, we are left with the evidence, from this mount, that tenure of the two named premises overlapped, and it would appear that this could only have occurred at some point between 1894 and 1899. This view of the picture's date is reinforced by the costumes that the women wear.

The small, firmly-centred hats belong to the nineties, but most readily datable of all are the leg-of-mutton sleeves worn by the two women on the right. Sleeves passed through a series of fashions in the nineties. First came sleeves pleated into the armhole to produce a 'kick-up' effect. In the middle of the decade the shoulder and upper sleeve billowed out before becoming tight over elbow and forearm, as worn by the younger women here. The

wide sleeves disappeared rather abruptly around 1897, and the final sleeve fashion of the decade may be seen in *Figure 30*. So about 1895 to 1897 would seem likely for this photograph.

It will be noted, though, that the women are not all dressed in the same style. Only the younger ones are keeping up with the latest trends. The more sober sleeves of the woman standing on the left are reminiscent of the eighties, and the mixture of materials and trimmings in the dress of the oldest woman seem almost to provide an echo of the seventies. Fashion-consciousness, as one might expect, appears to diminish with age. In the case of the baby, the fashion detail to notice is the white fur, which is what babies were routinely placed on from the nineties onward.

The studio has solid, unpretentious chairs and a pleasant enough carpet. The backcloth mixes, as so often, art and nature in its combination of foliage with architectural detail. It has, behind the woman in the pale dress, a neutral area for subjects to stand against. The number of subjects here, though, means that the framing effect has to be sacrificed and that the woman standing on the left has a series of verticals rising from her head. Fortunately the painting is rather muted, so the viewer's sense of shock is much reduced.

The grouping is partly strange. The baby, carefully supported but able to hold its own head up, is placed on furs in the centre. The young woman holding it, who is presumably its mother, directs her gaze at the child. The oldest woman, though she looks out of the picture at the camera, makes contact with furs and baby clothes with her left hand. But the two standing women are posed so as to relate to the others (and the photographer) as little as possible. One admittedly has a hand on a chairback, but both look out of the picture at different points from the older woman and each other. Neither relates to the baby at the centre of the picture.

I find myself trying to decide whether four or five generations are represented in this photograph. Are the two women on the right an older and younger sister? Is there really a generation between the two standing women? If there are five generations, then the adults must, working anti-clockwise from the baby, be aged about 20, 40, 60 and 80, or perhaps around 18, 36, 54 and 72. I find it hard to convince myself that their ages are thus spaced. But the Victorians enjoyed extremes and contrasts in pictures, and would have appreciated a photo which made a point about a series of generations. I am reluctant to give up the five generation theory entirely, simply because that might be the whole point of the exercise. If only four age groups are covered, why not leave out whichever is the odd women in the parent-child chain, and thereby preserve the clarity of the statement?

A medical footnote is offered. We should certainly be wary of diagnosing our ancestors' health problems on the evidence of old photographs. Many an apparent thyroid condition in early pictures is really no more than the fixed stare of one trying not to move or blink during a prolonged exposure. Nevertheless, it seems reasonable to conclude from the hands of the old lady in this picture that she suffered from arthritis.

Figure 30

A vignetted cabinet print by E Pannell, of 49 St George's Road, Brighton, provides a last look at the nineteenth century, and the woman's appearance is characteristic of its final years.

Since about 1890 skirts had become much plainer and the fashion emphasis had been focused on the upper half of the body. The leg-of-mutton sleeves, so popular in the middle of the decade, gave way very quickly around 1897 to close fitting sleeves with puffed shoulders, such as are seen here. The dress is trimmed across the bodice and at the cuffs with lace, which grew in popularity in the nineties and was to feature prominently on blouses and dresses of the 1900s. Standing collars, with or without pie-crust frills, were popular throughout the last twenty years of the century. The height of this late nineties' collar could hardly be greater. Men's high stand-up collars reached their 3" maximum in 1899, so some coincidence of male and female fashions can be observed here.

The decade saw some variety of women's hairstyles. If a bun was worn, it was generally caught up loosely at the back. The hair here has some height, but may be arranged over a pad before being drawn together behind. Whilst we cannot see the back of this woman's head, something like a ribbon protrudes from behind it to her right and would appear to be related to her hair rather than her paler collar. The curly fringe was a common sight in the eighties and was less common thereafter. But there were those who retained it. The lack of parting is characteristic of the nineties.

The vignette format is, of course, virtually diagnostic of the age, though here the medium-length shot and the restrained vignetting allow us to see cuffs, relaxed hands and opulently

padded chairback. The fading towards white begins, but is never fully achieved.

The woman's faint smile seems likely to be a natural expression, since fixed and inscrutable half-smiles were no longer a product of the need to keep still for a long time. Notice, though, that the smile is still a long way from a beam, and that the eyes are not focused on the camera. (If, incidentally, the eyes seem to be staring a little, it is the result of very pale irises which make her pupils seem, by contrast, very striking.) The smile, such as it is, is not directed at us, but arises from serene and beautiful inner thoughts. In the 1890s photographers were still looking to stereotype by age and sex, and the qualities suggested here are not significantly different from those suggested by *Figure 7*, which was taken some thirty years earlier.

The subject wears two rings on, intriguingly, the middle finger of her left hand. One can only wonder whether this departure from normal practice has anything to do with the hand itself. The knuckle of the forefinger looks very painfully swollen.

The mount ties in very happily with a dating of the late nineties. Its cream coloured card, now a little greyish, has slightly chamfered edges. The back is plain and smooth. The front is textured and the photographer's name and address, as well as the border lines within which the print has been stuck, have been pressed into the card. A rather pale brown ink has been used for the printing, and the tonal contrast between lettering and background is rather softer than it appears when the picture is reproduced in black and white. This is all a far cry from the black,

green, maroon and gold colour schemes that were in vogue for much of the nineties, and from the birds, flowers, cherubs and other images that adorned the backs of mounts. In fact, as the century drew to an end, many photographers reacted against excess and opted for a nouveau chaste style of mount. Portraits from the later nineties are quite often presented in a much more subdued setting. It is perhaps possible that the mount of *Figure 29*, with its cream, gold and brown palette, is another example of the new modesty, though the pictorial enthusiasm of the back makes me doubt it. But this cabinet print definitely speaks of a change in taste and provides an early example of the sort of matt and textured cream or pale grey mount that was to be common during the Edwardian period.

Figure 31

There are no problems with dating this photograph. As the writing at the bottom of the mount informs us, the date is 1901, and the subject is Freddy. Freddy is the baby, and the album from which this picture comes traces his growth for the first seven or eight years of his life, as well as containing a selection of other family pictures. Here Freddy is seen with his father outside the family home.

From its size, the picture appears to be a carte de visite, but it is one in a rather informal sense. By the turn of the century the carte had almost died out. Some were still being produced in the traditional way from glass negatives, but roll film quickly came to dominate in the new century. What we see here is a roll film picture that has been turned into a do-it-yourself carte. The print has been trimmed and pasted on to a piece of carte-sized cardboard. The mount is creamy white and bears no printing, but the fact that it has been commercially produced is shown by its bevelled, gilded edges. Mounts like this, whereby 'modern' photos could be made to slip neatly into the pre-cut apertures of existing albums, were clearly very

Freddy. 1901.

convenient. More or less makeshift cartes, and small photographs printed to finished carte size but unmounted, were still occasionally produced until the beginning of the Great War. They filled, quite literally, a small gap in the market. The alternatives were to cut larger pictures down to size, to put pictures into cabinet print apertures that were too

big for them, or to admit that the family album had outgrown its active life. Many family albums show some of these signs of compromise before one comes to the last few empty pages.

The picture is one of a pair that are mounted in this way. Mum, in her picture, holds Freddy. Dad, more restrainedly, stands by the pram. After all, he is a chap. The pram itself is a substantial affair — none of your flimsy carry-cots or baby-buggies of later years. It has decorated side panels and a jauntily curved handle. Nevertheless, this is a relatively sleek model, suitable for an older baby that can sit up by itself. The visible bedding appears to include the white fur which had become a necessary baby accessory in the 1890s.

Freddy's father is rather dashing. He has the high collar that came into fashion at the very end of the nineteenth century. The braid-trimmed jacket with frogging at the pockets is doubtless very natty, and it is only a cynical modern eye that would find it resembles a cut-down dressing-gown. He wears a homburg, a felt hat with indented crown. The homburg was not new on the scene, but it was becoming increasingly popular. Hats were still de rigueur out of doors, but the homburg and bowler were by now replacing the top hat. The homburg's name derived from that of a

German spa town much favoured by the Prince of Wales or, as he became during the year in which this picture was taken, King Edward VII. Notice the slightly rakish angle of the hat, and the cigar in the mouth. The cigar points straight at the camera, so is foreshortened, but it is there. Roll film, recording people out of doors, ushered in an age of pictures of people smoking. This was to build up and continue, without class distinction, for over half a century.

The print has deteriorated somewhat. There has been some fading, and there is some orange-tinged mottling in the shadows on either side of the hat. This mottling, which is more extensive on the companion picture, may be the result of rusting of metal particles in the original emulsion. This does not, however, help with identifying the photographic process, since such deterioration could occur to more than one.

The image, though, is not unsuccessful. By the turn of the century well-lit scenes could be given very short exposures, and baby photography could be tackled with some assurance. Here there is strong sunlight, as can be seen from the shadows on the steps and on the father's jacket, and Freddy has been caught naturally and mid-expression. The photographer may, of course, be Freddy's mother. Whoever it was seems to have come sensibly close to the subject, though it is impossible to be sure just how much the picture has been cut down. One can only observe that it is a little smaller than the accompanying Freddy and mother print, which may well also have been cropped. The background is of some importance, since the pair have been photographed outside the family home. A house, of course, provided an obvious and readily available background once people started to take their own photos and found they had to move outside to do so. But the threshold also constituted the family's face turned towards the world. It was popular not just as a background, but also as a subject in its own right. This family's front door and porch appear a number of times in their album, showing the world the kind of imposing villa that Ma and Pa could run to.

Figure 32

This fading, glossy photograph has been printed out as a postcard. Pictorial cards were first sent through the post in Britain in 1894, about twenty years after this means of communication had been established in the United States. The earliest examples appeared in various sizes, but by the turn of the century the most common size of card was 5½" by 3½", which is just what this one measures.

Until 1902 the picture and/or message appeared on one side and the whole of the back had to be reserved for the address. Then the divided back was introduced and messages were permissible on the right hand side only, and only for inland postage. By 1907 the combination of message and address on the back was also possible for a number of overseas destinations. Thus the printing on the reverse of this postcard gives a pretty clear indication of date, though it should first be pointed out that what we think of as the back was what our ancestral Post Office thought of as the front. The front of this postcard (or back, to our way of thinking) is divided, and to the left is printed, "This space, as well as the back, may now be used for communication but for inland only." This wording immediately suggests the period between 1902 and 1907.

But we can do a little better than that. It is the word "now" that is significant. "Now" implies novelty, and people soon get used to novelty. So, from about 1904 onwards the inclusion of "now" in the wording became less frequent. There was no sudden change, and it naturally took time for stocks of "now" cards to be used up, but it is fair to say that, within the period possible for this postcard, 1902 to 1905 is a little more likely than 1906/7.

Discussion of what was permitted through the post should not be allowed to obscure the fact that many postcards were never meant for sending. The postcard became a standard format for the printing of photographs, especially by professionals.

Whether this is a professional or amateur photograph is hard to say for sure. It certainly has an amateur air. The picture has been printed a long way off-centre, and a carpet has been hung up to provide a background, though it doesn't quite hide the brick wall and window behind. Makeshift backcloths were often attempted by amateurs, with a sheet proving perhaps the favourite resource. But turning back-yard or alley into a substitute studio was also the forte of the itinerant street photographer. Cloths or curtains could be stretched across a space or hung on a wall, and chairs, or even ornaments, could be brought out of doors to complete the picture. This photograph could be the work of such a practitioner.

It may be that the people who are pictured were not well off, and would have had to think twice about employing a studio professional. The picture is definitely Edwardian, dating from 1902 at the earliest, but the woman holding the child is still dressed partly in the fashions of around 1895, for she has leg-of-mutton sleeves.

Other fashion details, though, are firmly of the Edwardian age. Blouses were popular from about 1890, but enjoyed even greater favour in the early years of the new century, when they could be very elaborate lace-bedecked items. But the floppy waists, worn here by the figures in the back row, were to disappear around 1908. The fact, incidentally, that the two at the back are dressed alike, must mean that they are sisters. The hats speak resoundingly of the early 1900s. The broad-brimmed hat with flat and decorated crown (looking rather like a gateau on a plate) was typical and is clearly illustrated here. The three women in the front row look as if they have jointly entered a fancy dress competition and gone as a sweet trolley.

Figure 33

The reference to the king at the bottom of this cabinet print immediately gives an earliest possible date of 1901. Frederick Ralph, not the only Ralph to practise along the Wash-side coastal strip in the early twentieth century, had a studio in seaside Hunstanton. But it is his operations in nearby Dersingham which supply the explanation of his royal patronage, for Dersingham is next door to Sandringham.

This, then, must be a rather late example of the cabinet print, and the mount shows those signs of rediscovered simplicity that are often a feature of late examples. It is of matt, cream card, with brown printing on the front and no printing at all on the back.

The woman's clothes are of their age. The blouse and skirt combination, having gained some popularity in the nineties, came into its own with the new century. The long, loose sleeves fastened tightly at the wrist, and the contrast between simple full length skirt and lacy, decorated blouse are typical of the 1900s. The floppy waist of the blouse, like those seen in *Figure 32*, discourages us from putting the picture later than about 1908. The big hat is assertively Edwardian.

Thus evidence from the front of the picture suggests that we are firmly into the new century, whilst being at least a couple of years short of its second decade. It is satisfying, therefore, to turn over the print and see, hand-written on its otherwise plain back, "taken July 1906. Rosa".

The flowery glade backdrop seems to have been quite common at this time. The rather indistinct, slightly faded look of the foliage is not the result of any problem with depth of focus or lighting. There does seem to have been a tendency in late Victorian and Edwardian studios towards faintly

F. Ralph,

BY SPECIAL APPOINTMENT
TO
H.M. THE KING.

HUNSTANTON & DERSINGHAM.
NORFOLK.

impressionistic backgrounds, suggesting a context for the subject without insisting on that context by too much emphasis on detail. There is still some of the tolerance of incongruity that has been noticed before in studio settings. So the sylvan dell, like so many sylvan dells before it, comes complete with furniture. On this occasion the chosen item is a rather knobbly version of the kind of cane furniture that was popular. The table's rustic credentials, though, are established not just by its knobbliness, but also by a handful of flowers and curled leaves strewn on the top.

There is, however, one advance in the direction of verisimilitude. The division between ground and backcloth has become much less clear. Gone is the undisguised and unembarrassed line of demarcation where foliage was wont, in so many Victorian settings, to turn abruptly into carpet or lino. The floor here has a non-committally textured look, and Rosa has been placed well back, close to the backcloth, so the sense of visual continuity into the depths of the scene is quite strong. It would be wrong to claim that all Edwardian studios showed a new concern for realism in backcloths. The close-up vignettes of the 1890s had perhaps weakened the backcloth tradition anyway, and many photographers seem to have been making little or no use of them by this time. But a similar concern for the preserving of illusion, though using a very different backcloth, may be seen in *Figure 35*.

Cameras were, by 1906, quite capable of capturing smiles. *Figure 31*, taken five years earlier, shows that even an amateur could catch the fleeting expression of that traditionally difficult subject, a baby. But Rosa offers a solemn face to the world. Whilst the snapshot era was to usher in an age of grins, in themselves no more natural than the sober stares of the past, the studio still leaned towards decorum. Serious features by now had more to do with values than with exposure times.

Figure 34

This Edwardian photograph measures 3" by 5" and has been pasted into a postcard-sized space on a creamy-white, matt card. The mount brings the finished item, as it now appears, up to a size a little smaller than cabinet print. But it was once larger. The central postcard shape is pressed into the card. Around that is a smooth, raised border, and an imprinted, textured border surrounds that. At this point the card has been trimmed, in a rather wobbly fashion, to fit into an album or, perhaps more probably, a frame. How much cardboard has been trimmed away is not known, but many studio photographs of this era show a taste for a fairly extensive area of mount to set off the image.

On the back of the mount are listed just some of the USA studios, which formed a successful chain in the years before the Great War, and at one of which this picture was taken. Eight addresses in the London area are mentioned and five in the provinces. One of the provincial addresses is Orford Place, Norwich, and 1908 marks the only appearance of this studio so far found in trade directories up to and including 1916. Somewhere around the end of the century's first decade would seem, on this evidence, to be a likely date.

The woman's appearance would support this dating, for women's hats were at about their biggest from around 1908. One reason for enormous hats was enormous hairstyles. Hair was built up high on the head and needed something pretty spacious to accommodate it. This picture actually gives us the opportunity to look up under the brim and see that the hat appears almost to float on top of the hair in a manner reminiscent of a lampshade fixed over a bulb.

Other fashion details are also Edwardian. Collars, generally high and pie-crusty since the 1880s, remained so until the arrival

of the V-neck shortly before the war. Sleeves were generally tight at the wrist, and often fuller above. Bell-shaped skirts were standard for the first eight to ten years of the century, before the arrival of the closer fitting dresses and hobble skirts of the early Georgian years. There was lots of use of white and pale pastel colours, that created the kind of cool look which we see in this picture, and which nostalgia has incorporated into its wistful image of a decade-long, slightly out-of-focus, Edwardian summer.

The simple metal-framed spectacles, though, are of a style that can be seen in photographs ten, twenty and thirty years earlier.

The studio has some air of a new age about it. Though the use of backcloths was by no means over, many photographers were settling for a plain and uncluttered context for their sitters. The background here is not uniform, but it is simple and undistracting. The seat has something of the cool elegance of the dress and has a feeling of art nouveau — especially the less florid idiom of Charles Rennie Mackintosh, who was active at the time of this photograph.

On the face of it, the pose remains pretty traditional. Elbow rests on furniture and head on hand in traditional ladylike pose. But the gaze, though serious, is direct, and there is a casualness in the arm stretching out along the back of the seat. I may be looking too hard for signs of the New Woman, but it seems to me that there is more here of the ease and assurance found in such pictures of men as *Figures 9* and *12*, than of the demure pensiveness seen in, say, *Figure 23*.

The bloom, or metallic sheen of silver particles, that was found on *Figure 13*, is also present in the darkest areas of this photograph. This indicates that the picture has been printed on paper with a gelatine-based emulsion. One of the post-1903, so-called 'self-toning' papers seems possible since these were sometimes produced with a lightly tinted base, which could account for the creamy (rather than either white or yellowed) highlights of the picture.

Figure 35

This photograph of a soldier is presented in postcard format. The studio is identified as Garrison and Deakin of 14 St George Gate, Doncaster, and hand-written on the back is "For. Fred". Though printed for mailing on the reverse, this, like vast numbers of such pictures, was never likely to pass through the postal system. The postcard had become the standard studio format, just as cartes and cabinet prints had been in their day.

Only in the case of early postcards do printed instructions about postal regulations provide much help with dating. This example bears three instructions on the back: "This Space for communication", "The Address to be written here" and, in a suitably shaped box, "Stamp here". After 1907 instructions sometimes listed parts of the world for which the communication space might be used, but quite often they became as simple as they are here. So lack of reference to regulations merely means the card is not earlier than 1907. Sometimes the amount of postage required was printed in the stamp box, with a halfpenny being due until 1918, when the amount rose to a penny. Often though, as in this case, price was not mentioned.

In fact, this is an occasion when the subject effectively dates the picture. Pictures of soldiers off to war or home on leave abound, and examples appear in many family collections. Broadly speaking, studio portraits seem more likely to be deliberate souvenirs prior to first departure than snatched photos arranged during a brief leave. Snapshots could, of course, be taken at virtually any opportunity. The emotional need of relatives to have a picture of the young man leaving to face unknown dangers is apparent enough. What, with hindsight, is often disturbing about these pictures, especially the roll-film examples, is the carefree mood of the young men they depict.

This soldier, though, is no new recruit. He is a sergeant. Since it has often been the function of photography to mark important stages in our passage through life, it is quite possible that this picture was taken to commemorate the subject's acquisition of his third stripe. His uniform seems to be a rather better fit than is often seen on recruits, and he has the gravity and the manly stance to go with his rank.

The arms-folded stance was useful with men of action. It provided something to do with the hands when the normal contrivances were inappropriate. A book, after all, would have seemed too contemplative and an umbrella too effete, whilst uniforms and sporting wear offered no lapels to hold on to. Thus, soldiers and sportsmen tended to fold their arms a lot or, sometimes, if seated, place their hands flat on their knees. Indeed, for team photographs the convention is not yet entirely dead.

It is hard to say much about the soldier's appearance. His haircut and moustache are of the period, though not exclusively so. Tunic and long gaiters, rather than battle-dress blouse and short gaiters, tell us which World War we should be thinking of. It may be that there are details of uniform that would be eloquent to those who are expert in such things, but the signs are unpromising, as there is no shoulder flash, arm badge or cap badge to pin down the unit.

The backcloth shows that, despite such examples as *Figure 34*, there was still some taste for such things. It's rather nicely done. I'm not quite sure that the perspective of the stairs is entirely right, but I'm not quite sure either that it isn't. It carries the suggestion of a dramatic entrance having just been effected. The curtain is part of the painting, as can be seen from some very bold brushwork in the folds at the bottom. But what is not evident is the traditionally obvious line between cloth and floor. Where exactly does the one start and the other finish? The bottom line of the bottom stair would seem to offer the natural join line, but the painted curtain comes down further than that. The camouflaging of the meeting point has become of interest in a way that it never used to be.

Figure 36

This photograph simply has "Post Card" and, in the appropriate places, "Communication" and "Address Only" printed on the back.

It shows a street party, and there is not much difficulty in deciding what is being celebrated. Union Jacks could be used for any national event, and the event must, from the dress and faces of many of the adults, be a happy one. The coronation of George V would be too early for the appearance of a Chaplin look-alike, since his first films were not made until 1914. There would, indeed, be no point in dressing up as him until he had become very well known, which pushes the date a few years later. The number of uniforms and part uniforms in the picture force us to think in martial terms. The event has, of course, to be the end of World War I, which was accompanied by great outbursts of street partying.

The big occasion for celebration was not, in fact, the Armistice of 11th November 1918, but the signing of the Peace Treaty at Versailles on 28th June 1919. History subsequently settled down to commemorate the earlier date — rather more reasonably, since the treaty of Versailles lasted only a little time, whilst the desire to remember the war and be thankful for its end survived. So we may put this picture at the end of June 1919 with some confidence. The facts that greenery was freely available to make garlands (above the flags and paper flowers on the houses), that some of the flowers below the main hangings on the left may be real, and that other pictures in the set from which this comes show trees (of which only one trunk is visible here) in full leaf, all support the presumption of a summer rather than a November date.

The picture is full of interesting detail and cries out for the use of a magnifying glass.

Many of the adults are in fancy dress. Charlie Chaplin, whose imitator is at the centre of the picture, was by this time a household name. He had completed all his Essanay films and had made such well known titles as *Easy Street*, *The Immigrant* and *Shoulder Arms*, in which he had figured as the Little Man in uniform. The war years saw him at the height of his popularity, with cinemas in the United States holding look-alike competitions, and with him featuring on the front page of the English comic, *Funny Wonder*. This will not have been the only street party at which he was impersonated.

Other costumes include a pierrot, a bear and another animal skin, the wolfish snout of its head peeping out from under its wearer's arm. There are a number of uniforms, or bits of uniform, some of which must also qualify as fancy dress, since they have been appropriated by women. Another woman sports a top hat and bow tie. Scattered amongst uniform caps we see a trilby or two, the ubiquitous and classless boater, some sorts of ethnic headgear, an example, on the extreme left, of the sort of woman's hat that was common before the war, and one or two pieces of headwear that defy categorisation. A man at the back, on the right, appears to be wearing a mask that would suit the Phantom of the Opera and a wig that would do very well for Worzel Gummidge.

We can pick out a nurse and two musicians. The instrumentalist next to the bear is easy to find, but the folds of the accordion of the trilby wearer at the back are only just visible between the heads of those in front of him. Another picture from the same set shows that a harmonium had also been brought out on to the street. At least one man is smoking a cigarette, and another has a pipe. (Pictures of women smoking did not, by and large, start appearing until the twenties.)

The children, three of whom have large turned-down collars worn, in the Harrovian style, outside the jacket, are seated for the party tea. Their chairs have been brought out from houses all along the street, and so appear in a variety of styles. The youngsters look rather dubious. They perhaps have less cause than the adults to understand what the celebrations are all about. They could also be a little bewildered by the uncharacteristic behaviour and dress of the adults around them.

The grown-ups look as if they are really in festive mood. At least, most of them do. Perhaps I am just imagining that one or two of the men, unable to erase the recent past from their memories, cannot shake off a certain haunted look. One should beware of becoming too fanciful. I suppose. Most of the adults, at any rate, are unfeignedly happy to celebrate the end of the war to end all wars. We, with hindsight, might add, "Until the next one." But they are protected from such thoughts, safe within their moment of history.

Cover Photograph

The studio setting for this photograph could quite easily be late Victorian. The textured, weathered balustrade is reminiscent of the stonework in *Figure 28*. The fairly impressionistic foliage of the backcloth is balanced by some of the genuine article at the bottom of the picture and just appearing in-frame at the right. This could well belong to any period from the 1880s on.

The presentation, however, encourages us to think of the early years of the twentieth century. The picture is noticeably smaller than a postcard and coincides with neither of the standard Victorian formats. It is set on a mount of creamy white card which has a slightly rough texture to its outer border and a slightly indented central area for the photograph itself. The printing, which tells us that the studio was run by J. Weston and Son at 20a Sandgate Road, Folkestone, is fairly small and unassertive. The crown, with the words 'Patronised by Royalty', offers a muted echo of the self-proclamations of earlier years, but the overall effect is restrained. The mount has the sobriety that began to appear in the late 1890s, and which is especially characteristic of the Edwardian age.

The clothes and hair confirm the suggested dating. Lace-trimmed blouses reached their height of popularity in the early 1900s, and the taste for curved or V-shaped panels hanging at the front is sometimes also seen in dress design of these years. It fits in with the heavy-bosomed look that found favour. Whilst sleeves had lost the various kinds of upper-arm extravagance characteristic of the 1890s, a fullness towards the wrist, ending in a close-fitting cuff, is often seen in photographs and illustrations from this time.

Hair drawn onto the top of the head, but allowed some fullness rather than pulled tight, also ties in with the Edwardian years.

The pose has a pensiveness that is familiar from earlier days, and the placing of the right arm and hand is entirely traditional. Nevertheless, the gaze is directed towards the camera, and there is a pleasing feeling of assurance that is reminiscent of *Figure 34*, and of coolness that may be enhanced by the pale irises. The left hand has a ring on the third finger, and it is this, carefully displayed, which may be the picture's real subject. There was still the tendency to go to a studio for engagement and wedding portraits (though photos of outdoor wedding groups became increasingly common during Edward's reign).

The picture's apparently full range of grey tones makes me wonder whether it is a platinum print. This process, introduced around 1880, and popular until the Great War, achieved some subtlety in the rendering of tonal qualities. I am hesitant to push the claim, though, because a really close study of the print's surface is impossible.

Something sad has happened. Somebody at a later date has, with no doubt the best of intentions, had a go at laminating the photograph. A piece of self-adhesive plastic has been stuck over the image. It hasn't been cut very accurately, so it is 4 millimetres wider at the top than at the bottom, and it is somewhat smaller than the mount. But it completely covers the image. It is therefore impossible to see whether the picture's surface is matt (which I suspect) or glossy, and the subtle grey tones I referred to are overlaid with yellowing plastic.

Contact with certain plastics, PVC especially, can be harmful to photographs, and adhesives can stain. In this case, dust has stuck to the adhesive at the edges, where the plastic has been cut, and has created a dark line. The picture is dying. I don't know how long it will last, but already there is some discoloration, in addition to that of the laminating material, below the right eye. The plastic cannot be removed without damaging the image to which it is stuck. The best that can be hoped is that deterioration is slow, and the sensible course would be to make a copy quickly.

The warning to us all is clear. Old photographs, and new ones, need to be looked after. The simplest rule is never do anything to a photograph that can't be undone. There are many photographs around that are already much older than any of us. With care, most of them should last a lot longer still. But they do need a little kindness.

Afterword

Little remains to be said. Some conclusions will have been drawn and interpretations offered by which the reader is not convinced. There will doubtless be moments of questionable judgement or disputed reading of evidence. The business of dating and commentary is no exact science. It might just be less interesting if it were.

It would be foolish to claim that there is more in old photographs than meets the eye. There is in them precisely that which does meet the eye. But I think the eye benefits from a little thoughtful practice at recognising what meets it. Such practice on my part has formed the bulk of this small book. The hope is that readers will have shared the practice, and will go on to enjoy some more practising on their own.

Old family photographs provide the obvious place to start, but once you have the habit, you may find yourself applying it to any examples that you come across. Illustrations in books, pictures in museums, even advertisements for restoration and copying in photographers' shop windows can set the curious mind to dating and interpreting. You may also discover yourself looking at period costume and settings in films with newly opened eyes. Broadly speaking, since the late 1960s and early 1970s, increasing care has been taken over authenticity. In some earlier productions for the cinema, however, you many find leg-of-mutton sleeves chosen to represent a far larger chunk of history than they actually took up in real life.

The fact remains that, for most people, the family album (or shoe box) will provide the main material for investigation, and that is where the initiative passes to the reader.

Enjoy your old photographs. And remember, the more you look, the more you see.

Bibliography

Much fuller and more balanced bibliographies for the student of early photography may be found in *Dating Old Photographs* and *Understanding Old Photographs*. The intention here is to list those books which I have consulted in drawing up notes on the casebook photos. They represent, simply, that selection from my own library that I have found it convenient to have to hand. Embarrassingly, my own earlier books are included, not because I wish here to make any special recommendation of them, but because I really have referred back to them, and especially to the charts in *Dating Old Photographs*. I hope, therefore, that my inclusion of them in this bibliography will be accepted as evidence less of arrogance than of fallible memory.

Appleby, David & John, *The Magic Boxes: Professional Photographers and Their Studios in North Essex 1845-1937*. Essex Record Office, 1992.

Cunnington, Phillis, *Costume in Pictures*. Studio Vista, 1964.

Dimond, Frances & Taylor, Roger, *Crown and Camera — The Royal Family and Photography*. Penguin, 1987.

Hallett, Michael (ed.), *Victorian and Edwardian Professional Photographers in Glasgow*. Royal Photographic Society (Historical Group), 1990.

Lansdell, Avril, *Fashion À La Carte 1860-1900*. Shire, 1985.

Lansdell, Avril, *Seaside Fashions 1860-1939*. Shire, 1990.

Laver, James, *Costume Through the Ages*. Thames & Hudson, 1963.

Laver, James, *A Concise History of Costume*. Thames & Hudson, 1969.

Linkman, Audrey, *The Victorians - Photographic Portraits*. Tauris Parke, 1993.

Pols, Robert, *Dating Old Photographs*. Countryside Books, 1993, & Federation of Family History Societies, (second edition) 1995.

Pols, Robert, *Understanding Old Photographs*. Robert Boyd, 1995.

Pritchard, Michael, *A Directory of London Photographers 1841-1908*. PhotoResearch, (revised edition) 1994.

I have also made use of my own unpublished directories of early photographic studios in Norfolk, Suffolk and Cambridgeshire.